H7

# THE FIRST
# EXPATRIATES

# THE FIRST EXPATRIATES

## Americans in Paris During the French Revolution

## YVON BIZARDEL

### Translated by
*June P. Wilson* and *Cornelia Higginson*

HOLT, RINEHART AND WINSTON
*New York*

Published simultaneously in Canada by Holt, Rinehart
and Winston of Canada, Limited.

Library of Congress Cataloging in Publication Data
Bizardel, Yvon.
The first expatriates.
Translation of Les Américains à Paris pendant la
Révolution.
Includes bibliographical references.
1. Americans in France. 2. France—History—
Revolution, 1789–1799. I. Title.
DC158.8.B5313      914.4′06′13      74-15482
ISBN 0-03-012421-2

First published in France under the title
*Les Americains à Paris pendant la Revolution*
by Editions Calmann-Levy S.A.
Additional materials for the English-language edition
by June P. Wilson.

*Allégorie Républicaine*, p. iii, courtesy the
French Cultural Service.
The detail of *La Promenade de la galerie du Palais Royal*,
p. 1, courtesy the Bibliothèque Nationale, Paris.

First Edition

Designer: Sandra Kandrac
Printed in the United States of America

# Contents

# Foreword

WHILE PREPARING A WORK ON AMERICAN PAINTERS IN PARIS,
I learned that artists such as John Trumbull and John
Vanderlyn, who was the first American student enrolled at
the Ecole des Beaux-Arts, were traveling in France during
the French Revolution. My research led to the discovery of
other United States citizens, not involved with painting, who
were living in Paris during this uneasy period. Few of those
names were familiar to me, aside from those of Admiral John
Paul Jones, who died in 1792 in an apartment on rue de
Tournon; Thomas Paine, who became a member of the
National Convention; Gouverneur Morris, the author of a
much celebrated diary; and Joel Barlow, who posed for
Houdon.

The others intrigued me. Who was William Short, the
secretary left in Paris by Jefferson in 1789, who for nearly
three years was the United States representative to a dying
French court? The memory of this well-meaning Virginian
might have faded from history were it not for his correspondence with Mme. de La Rochefoucauld, which spanned
nearly half a century and is now retained by the Philosophical Society in Philadelphia.

Who was James Swan, whose personal effects, furniture,

and vases from Sèvres, acquired in Paris during the Reign of Terror, are now in the possession of the Boston Museum? What about Gilbert Imlay, who in 1793 lured the British feminist Mary Wollstonecraft to the shadow of the guillotine?

Who were these unknown soldiers: George Schaffner, tied to Armand de La Roüerie by bonds of friendship as solid as a marriage and, like him, a Breton royalist; in the opposing camp, General John Skey Eustace of New York, engaged as a volunteer in the army of the Republic, and who belonged to the staff of Dumouriez?

Why did Nantucket whalers settle in Dunkirk and Lorient? Why was R. P. Chauvier, the father superior of the Mathurin friars, concerned with the redemption of American sailors captured by the Barbary pirates and sold as slaves in the Algerian marketplace?

In order to discover the answers to these troublesome questions, I undertook some new research.

At the outset, four sources provided me with nominative lists of Americans residing in Paris between 1789 and 1799. Both the papers of Thomas Jefferson and the letters and intimate diary of Gouverneur Morris enabled me to uncover the names of a great many people. Then, too, there were the signatures of famous Americans present in Paris during this period on the petition submitted to the Convention requesting the release of Thomas Paine, who was imprisoned in 1793. My final source was the letter sent by Americans in Paris to their representative, James Monroe, when he left his post in 1796.

Thanks to this basic list, which was further enriched by my studies, I managed to compile a "directory" of more than two hundred names. Few of these have been preserved in French history.

John Paul Jones has never been a legendary figure in France, and so none of the excellent studies published about him in the United States have been translated. As for Thomas Paine, he attracted some attention from English-language authors; but French historians barely mention Paine, apart from Edouard Herriot who devotes only one or two pages to him. Regarding Paine's works, which by 1792 were already so well disseminated in France that he was elected a member of the Convention, they have not been reissued in our language since 1822, when the editor Poulet published a final edition of *Common Sense.*

Gouverneur Morris, although esteemed by many French historians, has suffered from their naïveté. If Goncourt, Philarète Chasles, and Sainte-Beuve wronged him through their ignorance, the fault belongs to the carefully expurgated edition of Gouverneur Morris' *Journal*, which appeared for the first time in the United States in 1832, and subsequently in 1888. In the two partially translated French editions, the editors disguised the identity of the author and let it be known that his relations with Mme. de Flahaut, who at the time was Talleyrand's mistress, were strictly platonic.

America had to wait until 1939 to have the full text reconstructed from the first draft, but unlike the editions of 1839 and 1888, this later edition was not translated into French. Only one of our countrymen devoted an entire volume to Gouverneur Morris, in 1906. Unfortunately, the author, A. Esmein, encountered the same difficulties as his predecessors.

In conclusion, I wish to express my appreciation to the archivists and librarians who welcomed me as warmly in the United States as in France and London. They are too numerous for me to mention. However, I will make an exception in the case of Howard C. Rice, a longtime curator of rare books in the Princeton Library and author of scholarly studies on Franco-American relations in the eighteenth century. To him I owe my introduction into the incomparable world of Thomas Jefferson, whose memory is especially honored at Princeton University.

Y. B.

# I
# THE
# LAST YEARS
# OF THE
# ANCIEN REGIME:
# 1785–1791

# 1

DURING THE YEARS THAT THE AMERICAN REBELS WERE fighting their War of Independence, the center of Franco-American friendship had been Benjamin Franklin's house in Passy. When Franklin returned to America in 1785, Thomas Jefferson came to replace him as "Minister Plenipotentiary of the United States of America to His Very Christian Majesty."

America's new representative to the Court of Versailles was as interested in human activities as he was in ideas, with agriculture his prime concern and architecture a close rival. The infant nation demanded multiple talents of its founders, and Jefferson had them in good measure. Beyond that, he had a subtlety of mind equal to that of any Englishman or Frenchman.

In 1785 the Champs Elysées was bisected by the Chaillot Gate near the rue Neuve-de-Berry. Jefferson installed his legation at the intersection in a *hôtel particulier* built by Chalgrin for the Comte de Langeac, who had subsequently been obliged to put it up for rent.

The disposition of the house and grounds was such that the new minister was able to accommodate a wide variety of guests. One such was his private secretary, William Short, who became virtually a permanent resident. Like Jefferson, Short was a Virginian and a graduate of the College of William and Mary, where he had been one of the founders of Phi Beta Kappa. In Paris the young man soon found himself treated like a member of the family. Jefferson was a widower, as Franklin had been before him, and to keep him company he brought his two daughters to Paris. They, however, made few appearances at the Hôtel de Langeac. In conformity with the practices of the day, he entrusted them to the convent of Panthémont, whose mother superior accepted Protestant girls provided they came from distinguished foreign families. To visit the girls at their fashionable establishment across the Seine, their father would take the ferry at Les Invalides. When he was unable to make the trip, he sent William Short with messages and treats.

Lacking a wife to run the house, Jefferson assumed the task himself. And there, on the edge of the Champs Elysées, he lived as if he were a Virginia planter, and the *hôtel* a town house in Richmond or Williamsburg. M. Petit, his *maître d'hôtel*, supervised the actual running of the house, watching over the kitchens, wine cellar, and stables, keeping a sharp eye on the silver and linens, dealing with the tradesmen, and handling the accounts. His authority also took in the Swiss guard, the lackeys, and Jim, the black slave Jefferson had brought with him. Jim was a talented cook, and Jefferson, hoping to add to the young man's repertoire of Southern dishes, made arrangements with the chef of a French nobleman to initiate Jim into the rites of French cooking. Meanwhile, ears of incomparable corn from Cherokee country ripened in the Champs Elysées vegetable garden.

In this atmosphere redolent of Virginia, Jefferson set to

work with enthusiasm. His activities ranged from diplomacy to commerce and politics; he negotiated loans from Dutch bankers, arranged benefits for French veterans of the War of Independence, and paid advances to Houdon and Dupré for art he had commissioned. The problems of Franco-American trade tempted him into bold projects. One involved the city of Honfleur in Normandy, which he hoped to transform into a free port, thus making it a general rendezvous for American shipping. With the support of the Duc d'Orléans, Louis XVI's cousin, Honfleur was soon on the way to becoming a giant warehouse for Carolina rice and a rival to the English port of Cowes, to which the Charleston planters had been taking their custom. Of a quite different nature was the problem of ransoming his countrymen who, captured on the high seas by Barbary pirates, had been sold in the Algiers market. In these negotiations, he was aided by Father Chauvier of the Congregation of Mathurins, a religious order that specialized in the recovery of Christians sold into slavery by the infidels.

To find his way through the maze of court and city life, Jefferson relied on the good graces of the Marquis de Lafayette. The marquis's *hôtel* on the rue Bourbon was wide open to the ideas and men of the New World, and it furnished a harmonious complement to the Hôtel de Langeac. Both men shared the same interest in their two countries and in achieving an enduring alliance between them. Thanks to his double nationality and his loyalty to both, the marquis was eager to build the relationship on something firmer than mere gratitude or friendship. If his ideas seemed limited and admittedly materialistic, at least—in his view—they were more durable than the bonds of friendship. Under the gilt ceilings of his *hôtel*, his guests talked of whale oil and the price of tobacco as if they were shopkeepers on the rue Saint-Denis. The men in the ancestral portraits would have been hard put to believe their ears: they might have countenanced a discussion of the American debt or the exploitation of land in the New World, but to haggle over the price of cod and herring was to descend to the level of fishmongers and seemed proof that the world was indeed coming to an end.

The visitors to the Hôtel de Langeac were no less varied than the subjects discussed within its walls. As in Franklin's day, Paris was a stopping place for Americans of every stripe—businessmen, sailors, adventurers, and young men of good family on the first leg of a "grand tour" of Europe. One day it might be David Humphreys, in Europe ostensibly to negotiate trade agreements with various countries, but also to act as secret agent in London, Lisbon, and Madrid. A graduate of Yale, he had been General Washington's much beloved aide-de-camp. Although Humphreys was one of the irrepressible "Connecticut Wits," Jefferson saw fit to twit him for "his French airs, for bad poetry, bad prose, vanity, etc."

Another day, Thomas Barclay from Philadelphia, who had been a member of the Committee of Correspondence and was now American consul to France, would stop by en route to a special mission to the Sharif's court in Morocco. Or it might be Philip Mazzei, Jefferson's neighbor at Monticello who had left his native Italy to introduce the culture of grapes and olives into Virginia. With Condorcet's help, Mazzei had just finished the first definitive history of the United States written in French and was now an intelligence officer to Stanislas II of Poland. Yet another guest was Lewis Little-page, also a graduate of William and Mary. Littlepage, who had turned soldier of fortune, was, like Mazzei, in Stanislas' service. The two men were always eager to prolong their stay in Paris on their way to and from Poland.

Nostalgia drew a few of Franklin's former visitors back to the banks of the Seine. Thomas Paine returned, this time less as an apostle of liberty than as an inventor in search of a patent. With him he had brought blueprints for a metal bridge, the first of its kind, and Jefferson duly submitted his plans to the Académie des Sciences.

In Paine's wake came another inventor, James Rumsey of Maryland, a promoter of steamboats. Rejected by both his native country and Great Britain, he turned to Paris to seek Jefferson's help. To the American minister he explained that, whereas it would take horses twelve days to tow a barge up the Seine from Rouen to Paris, the time could be reduced to one or two days using a craft propelled by streams of water forced by steam through the stern of the vessel. Seduced once again, Jefferson introduced Rumsey to the same Académie des Sciences.

For his appearance before this learned company, Rumsey was obliged to dress in a black suit with a sword at his waist, a powdered wig on his head, and a three-cornered hat under his arm. These trappings seemed to him oddly suited to a discussion of steam navigation—as he later wrote to a friend—but his amusement quickly vanished when he had to confront the Abbé d'Arnal. That churchman had his own notions about steam engines and had no intention of letting a foreigner threaten his monopoly. Rumsey took on the scornful abbé and the dispute continued after the session's end. It might have gone on forever had death not suddenly intervened and carried the churchman off to a better world.

Two of the most curious persons to pass under Jefferson's

porte cochere were William Langborn and John Ledyard. Each harbored plans for solitary travel, and more ambitious even than Jean-Jacques Rousseau, both were determined to cover a sizable part of the globe on foot, reaching the Orient by way of Russia. Langborn, a Virginian, was "an odd one," in Lafayette's words. He had taken part in the Battle of Yorktown and finished the war with the rank of colonel. Infected with travel fever, he had broken out of his natural melancholy and resolved to see the world on foot before he turned forty.

Ledyard, a native of Connecticut, was already a seasoned traveler, having accompanied Captain Cook on his last voyage to the South Pacific. His journal of that trip had appeared in 1783. A happy-go-lucky sort of man, his friendly ways soon charmed Jefferson, Lafayette, and their circle, and his ideas for opening up trade with the Pacific Northwest intrigued the American minister. Jefferson not only arranged for his passport, he also interceded for him with Baron Grimm. Although the baron did inform Empress Catherine of Russia that an American wished to traverse her country on his way to the Orient, the Czarina replied that she thought Ledyard's project mad. Rebuffed but not dissuaded, Ledyard turned to John Paul Jones for help. Jones was then serving in Catherine's navy, but unfortunately for Ledyard, the admiral's Russian career was nearing its end. For all his victories against the Turks, he had run afoul of naval intrigues and secured the enmity of Catherine's lover and adviser, Potemkin. To political failure was added personal disgrace as Jones was accused of "violating the person of a young girl." Nothing, however, could discourage the ebullient Ledyard.

Carefully avoiding each other, Langborn and Ledyard set off on their separate ways, paying no heed to the fact that, since they were leaving at the same time and going in the same direction, their paths were bound to cross. The inevitable meeting took place in Denmark, and the gregarious Ledyard suggested they travel together to Saint Petersburg. Langborn rejected the proposition. Aware that Ledyard had decided to speed up his trip in order to reach Kamchatka sooner, Langborn improvised a detour through Lapland that would assure that their paths did not cross again. So, with a pack on his back, compass in his pocket, his dog at his heels, he turned his back on his countryman and started off.

Langborn got as far as Saint Petersburg and eventually made it back to France in 1793. Ledyard was not so fortunate: he reached remote Yakutsk in 1787, only to be arrested a few months later by the Czarina's police in Irkutsk on Lake Baikal and marched back to the Polish border. The following year, Jefferson was greatly saddened to learn from Thomas Paine that Ledyard had died in Cairo on the first leg of a trip into Africa in search of the source of the Niger.

Luckily for Jefferson, William Short was of a less adventurous nature and discharged his duties with care and devotion. As a conscientious Virginian suddenly launched into Paris life, he determined to learn French as quickly as possible. With this in mind, he moved to Saint-Germain-en-Laye, where he boarded with a simple provincial family named Royer. He shared their lives for several months, even to forming a tender attachment for the daughter of the house.

When he returned to Paris to take up his duties again, he was welcomed into the most prestigious salons, including those of Lafayette, the Duchesse d'Orléans, the Marquise d'Houdetot, Condorcet, Madame Tronchin, and the Countess of Albany—widow of the last Stuart pretender to the

English throne, who had taken up residence in Paris with the Italian poet Alfieri. Jefferson also introduced him to the Duchesse d'Anville at the Hôtel de La Rochefoucauld, and this was to have a profound effect on the young man's life.

At Jefferson's invitation, a noteworthy artist soon made his appearance on the Paris scene. For a young man not yet thirty, John Trumbull had had a turbulent career. Despite a strange cranial malformation and an injury to one eye, he had shown an early talent for art. The son of Governor John Trumbull of Connecticut, he wanted to study with Copley, but his father insisted he go to Harvard. Service in the war interrupted his studies; afterward, more determined than ever to become a painter, he went to London and began his apprenticeship in Benjamin West's studio. His career was again interrupted when he was imprisoned "on suspicion of treason"; the charge was thought to be in retaliation for Major André's hanging, and Trumbull was released through the efforts of Charles Fox and Edmund Burke. By the time he received Jefferson's invitation, he had finished his paintings of the Battle of Bunker Hill and the attack on Quebec. He was then at work on Cornwallis' surrender at Yorktown, and it was Jefferson's idea that the young man should paint from life the Frenchmen who had taken part in that historic battle. So he arranged that Lafayette, Rochambeau, Lauzun, de Grasse, d'Estaing, Chastellux, Fersen, and other veterans of the American war should sit for their portraits at the Hôtel de Langeac. It also crossed Jefferson's mind that a visit to Paris, with its royal galleries and private collections and with its infinite possibilities for meetings with well-known painters and sculptors, might round out Trumbull's artistic education, hitherto restricted to London.

Perhaps the most controversial figure to set up residence in Paris was Gouverneur Morris (his mother had been a French Huguenot, hence his peculiar Christian name). Morris was a man of noble bearing despite a missing leg, but his arrival gave Jefferson scant cause for rejoicing. The two men did not get along, and their political views were poles apart. Jefferson detected about Morris the unpleasant odor of a shady businessman and of a politician much too well disposed toward the British. Yet he was obliged to extend a polite welcome, for Washington had praised him in a letter saying: "You will find [him] full of affability, good nature, vitality & talents . . . [and] a deportment calculated to do credit to the national character. . . ." Morris was also the representative of Robert Morris, one of America's most eminent men of affairs.

The two Morrises were unrelated, having started life on different continents and eighteen years apart—Robert in Liverpool and Gouverneur in Morrisania near New York City. But as the colonies started on the road to independence, their careers became closely intertwined. Through his shipping and banking interests, Robert Morris had been one of the chief importers of arms and munitions for the rebel armies and had financed the Yorktown campaign single-handedly. In the difficult years that followed the Revolution, he was appointed virtual dictator of America's finances. Like so many businessmen of his day, he was a politician as well, and one of the most distinguished among an extraordinary group of men: he had served his apprenticeship as a delegate to the Pennsylvania Assembly, then went on to the Constitutional Convention, and was chosen Pennsylvania's first Senator. He and Roger Sherman of Connecticut were the only men to sign all three documents formalizing the birth of the Republic: the Declaration of Independence, the Articles of Confederation, and the United States Constitution. Eventually he was to overreach himself; in 1792, when his speculations in land collapsed, he triggered America's first financial panic.

Gouverneur Morris had an auspicious start in life. Son of Lewis Morris, who was the Second Lord of the Manor in Morrisania and another signer of the Declaration of Independence, Gouverneur graduated from King's College (later Columbia College) at sixteen and was admitted to the bar at nineteen. Then, in quick succession, he was named Westchester's representative to the first New York Congress, took part in the Constitutional Convention for New York and the Continental Congress that followed. Refused reelection in New York, he moved to Philadelphia, then capital of the new nation, and became an assistant to Robert Morris during the latter's tenure as Superintendent of Finance. Their business association started then, Gouverneur's star always ascending as Robert's gradually declined. In 1787 the younger Morris, a staunch Federalist, was elected to the Constitutional Convention, and two years later found himself in Paris on a staggering variety of errands. The young nation had a huge debt; its greatest asset was its acreage of vast land ripe for exploitation. Little wonder that so many of the Americans who filed through Paris were trying to sell land in the New World. Morris was no exception: the land Robert Morris had commissioned him to sell was in the region of the Saint Lawrence River. But land was only one of his preoccupations. He was also to work out the details of the tobacco trade with the *Fermiers-Généraux*, open up new markets in the Caribbean where the French were jealously guarding their monopoly over all commercial transactions, and contact financiers in London and Amsterdam to learn how repayment of the American debt was progressing in order, if possible, to encourage speculation.

Morris was to combine these financial and business activities with a secret mission that the American diplomats stationed in Europe found most offensive. Without the knowledge of the United States Senate, Washington had asked Morris to go behind the backs of the ministers accredited to the courts of Versailles and St. James and give his own assessment of French and British attitudes toward the United States. Washington reasoned that in this way he would be able to compare private reports from an unofficial source with the formal reports of his ambassadors.

It did not take Jefferson long to pierce Morris' double role. He was well aware that the newcomer had direct access to Washington's ear and that he was passing along highly biased information. Morris had no sooner arrived than he asked Jefferson to present him to the foreign ambassadors; the other as quickly declined, on the pretext that the diplomatic corps was a waste of time. Jefferson, who considered Morris nothing more than a schemer, had no intention of gratifying his ardent desire for entrée to the court and Parisian society. Seeing that it was useless to insist, Morris turned to easier prey—the Marquis de Lafayette, who was always obliging where Americans were concerned. With Lafayette's help, the doors of the Paris salons swung open and Morris was soon cutting a brilliant figure. His promising debut was marred by the faux pas of calling on Fanny de Beauharnais, a bluestocking frowned on by the best society. But he quickly sized up the unfortunate countess and her little band of writers, which ran the gamut from Restif de la Bretonne to her current lover, Dorat-Cubières, and he fled

13

her house on the rue de Tournon, never to return. Instead, he found refuge in higher spheres where his impressive stature caught Houdon's eye on their first meeting, and his gallantry assured him the ladies' favor despite his wooden leg. In no time, he was admitted into the most aristocratic circles, including the salon of the Duchesse d'Orléans, a princess of the royal blood. The fledgling had only to try his wings to find himself securely perched at the summit.

If Gouverneur Morris gave Jefferson wide berth, other American expatriates in Paris besieged him with their tales of woe, and he in turn aided and abetted their projects. Many were veterans of the Revolutionary War, men like Colonels James Swan and Samuel Blackden. Originally a Scotsman from Fifeshire, Swan had won his rebel's spurs at the Battle of Bunker Hill. During the period of "idleness and extravagance which had succeeded the close of the war" (in Washington's words), Swan joined the growing list of speculators and managed to squander his wife's money on land in Pennsylvania, Virginia, and Kentucky. To make up for his losses, he joined the exodus to Paris. In no time he was recognized as "the chief American merchant" in the French capital. As for Blackden, he was in Paris to sell Kentucky land and to promote trade between the two countries.

Jefferson shared the two men's desire to see the United States more closely allied with the monarchy of Louis XVI so that France might take England's place in commercial relations with America. Their pragmatic minds were not filled with the philosophy of the day (though they were disciples of the Encyclopedists without knowing it). The horrors and abuses of the old system may have driven their ancestors from Europe and set a new generation of Americans against the British Crown, but once the curtain had come down on their revolution, these same Americans expected much from the French monarchy. In their eyes, the monarchy was making a judicious return to a state of order—an impression that might have been the result of their particularly skewed experience in France. For most of these men were Freemasons, and their experience of fraternity in the French Masonic lodges reinforced their faith in the destiny of France. This predisposition was not unmixed with down-to-earth considerations: an orderly and more prosperous France would mean increased trade across the Atlantic— a view shared by well-informed people on both sides of the ocean. Once the anticipated free trade reforms had had their effect on French economic expansion, the American importers, exporters, financiers, and shipowners in France would find themselves in highly favorable positions. As things stood now, they were suffering under a system so archaic that, despite their Francophile leanings, they were forced to take their banking business to London, Amsterdam, and Hamburg.

As the omens multiplied, the actors in the drama took their places on stage. Grouped around Lafayette, Brissot, and countless other sympathizers, the Americans awaited the coming of free trade, freedom of the high seas, and freedom itself.

Meanwhile, a certain American from Philadelphia was living a squire's life in a Brittany manor. His name was George Schaffner, and his presence in the region of Fougères might have gone unnoticed had he not chosen to throw in his lot with the Marquis de La Roüerie, whose escapades had long been the subject of local gossip.

La Roüerie's early career was like that of a hero in an Abbé Prévost novel. While an officer in the French Guards, he had snatched an opera singer from the arms of a septuagenarian, and after taking the stage to be applauded with his conquest, threatened to kill himself because of a broken heart. Another scrape had led to a duel: his adversary was left to bleed to death, and La Roüerie fled to Geneva to escape the King's justice. Finally he turned to the Trappists, hoping to find consolation in religion, "an adventure which caused much comment at the time," in the words of the diarist François de Bachaumont.

The monastery was no better able to restrain the scoundrel than the army. By the time the American colonies were rising against Great Britain, he was back on his estate. The sound of the shot heard round the world offered a welcome contrast to his dull existence at the manor with an unsympathetic mother and hostile neighbors who locked up their daughters when he came in sight. Nothing, not even Armand, the bastard child who bore his name, could keep La Roüerie at home: America called, and he answered.

The future revolutionary was the first Frenchman to embark, anticipating even Lafayette. He quickly dropped his title, switched identities, and became M. Armand. However, being fond of his creature comforts, he brought along his three favorite valets to see to his horses and person. In another era, he would have won his laurels in the Holy Land; in the year 1778, he embraced the popular cause of the moment, which happened to be liberty.

The New World satisfied his appetite for adventure, and he returned to France five years later a brigadier general in the American cavalry, highly pleased with himself and the republic he had helped to create. The Cross of Cincinnatus gleamed on his chest, and on that of the comrade he brought back with him. "He foraged about in the forests of Brittany," wrote Chateaubriand, "with an American major and a monkey perched on the rump of his horse." The American was George Schaffner.

According to a neighboring lady, La Roüerie "idolized" this American of humble birth, and even she was quite impressed with Schaffner's proud bearing. "I have heard it said that he is very witty," she noted in her diary, "but one has to guess at it as his French is very bad."

The two men were inseparable, joined by a vow never to part. Schaffner was La Roüerie's shadow. Leaving the monkey behind, they abandoned the château for a stay in Paris. La Roüerie used the visit to demand from Jefferson the back pay still owed him by the United States and to entreat Versailles to reinstate him in the King's army. This latter request was met with silence, for Ségur, the Minister of War, had no desire to see the hothead in His Majesty's officer corps.

Always out of pocket, La Roüerie decided that a rich marriage was the only solution to his difficulties. Having consistently struck terror in the hearts of fathers, he tried his luck with a widow, the Marquise de Saint-Brice; after much hesitation on the lady's part, he won the hand of her only daughter.

The bride took her place at the château between the two inseparables. Another guest soon joined them, a young doctor of the region summoned by the marquis to minister to his wife's delicate health. The marquise languished through the winter; come spring, Dr. Chevetel prescribed a watering place for his patient and offered personally to supervise her treatments at Cauterets in the Pyrenees so that La Roüerie and Schaffner could continue their escapades unhampered. Besides, the marquis was involved in the vast project of razing his château in order to build a new one on its site.

Dr. Chevetel returned from the Pyrenees alone; six short months after her wedding day, the marquise breathed her last. The widower had meanwhile decided to go on a trip to Germany to study Frederick the Great's military innovations, and he asked the Marquis de Chastellux, another veteran of the American war, to put in a good word for him with the King's ambassador in Berlin. Chastellux dutifully wrote: "We were together three years in America where he commanded a legion and was given the rank of brigadier general as a well-deserved reward for his distinguished services. He will be making the trip with M. Schaffner, a fine young officer who was a major in his legion."

The marquis moved to Paris with Schaffner and devoted what time was left over from his pleasures to preparations for the trip to Berlin. But he soon succumbed to the temptations of the capital: an actress named Mlle. Fleury had him so firmly entrapped that all thoughts of Frederick the Great and the Prussian army vanished from his mind. Confined to the wings, the faithful Schaffner watched as Mlle. Fleury took precedence over the trip across the Rhine. He would bide his time: before long, the horseback rides and the tête-à-têtes would resume. In the meantime, he spent his time eavesdropping in the cafés and gardens of the Palais Royal. In anticipation of a new day, Paris was polishing the phrases that would soon be used to proclaim its grievances; subversive pamphlets, songs, and epigrams circulated everywhere. The marquis explained the political subtleties that escaped Schaffner, and with such a teacher, the student made quick progress. From La Roüerie, he learned the grievances of the

Breton nobility, for, in addition to those of Frenchmen in general, the Bretons had a few of their own. The dukes, nobility, parliament, and top clergy of Brittany were out-shouting the rabble in their demands for a restoration of "Breton freedoms" and a return to the vanished days of the dukedoms. Stretching a point, they made their own use of the word "liberty." Why look further when such a magical term was at hand? Fighting for liberty, be it American or Breton, was the order of the day. What did it matter if the two conceptions of the word were poles apart?

Backing their rebel parliament, the Bretons rioted in Rennes to demonstrate their opposition to royal despotism, and the gentry egged them on in the name of local tradition. The heady smell of discord filled their nostrils; parley followed parley, culminating in a written protest. La Roüerie was an impassioned participant in the agitation and commu-nicated his ardor to Schaffner, who duly agreed that Versailles was exercising intolerable constraints against his adoptive province.

Since La Roüerie was in the thick of the intrigue, it was natural that he be one of the twelve gentlemen chosen by his peers to place the *Mémoire au Roi*, which listed their griev-ances, in Louis XVI's hands. While awaiting His Majesty's pleasure and their summons to Versailles, the twelve men met in Paris and organized a banquet to pass the time and nourish their enthusiasm. Shortly past midnight and the last toast, the marquis and his companion returned to their rooms at the Hôtel des Asturies in the Faubourg Saint-Germain. There, a band of police agents lay in wait to carry La Roüerie off to the Bastille, where at three in the morning he was joined by the eleven other deputies. Thus ended the Adventure of the Twelve Barons, while Schaffner, a Breton

19

by adoption only, was left behind at the Hôtel des Asturies.

Lafayette immediately took up the prisoners' cause and protested against the court's treatment of the Breton delegation. The Queen seized the occasion to ask what this marquis from the Auvergne had to do with Breton grievances, and as the regal frown was not lost on the court, Lafayette was removed from his army post.

Paris, however, had heard his protestations; the public's concern forced the governor of the Bastille to notify the police: "A large crowd assembles in the rue Saint-Antoine, on the boulevard, and in the rue Contrescarpe whenever the Breton gentlemen take the air on the towers or in the garden." Not unexpectedly, the American colony in Paris was also incensed at ex-Colonel Armand's arrest, and Jefferson reported it to his government.

Joel Barlow was perhaps the most engaging American to come to Paris during this entire period. Gay and witty, a poet, editor, lawyer, and briefly a minister, he was an odd choice to be Paris representative of the Scioto Company (named after the Scioto River, a tributary of the Ohio). What was a versifier doing beguiling prospective emigrants with the charms of Ohio real estate and selling them plots at advantageous prices? It was William Duer who had picked him for the job, and Duer had business acumen enough to float a dozen poets. Even Washington had written Lafayette by way of introduction: "Mr. Barlow is considered by those who are good judges to be a genius of the first magnitude." In any event, William Duer could do no wrong. The son of a British aristocrat, he had gone to India with Clive, turned up in America in 1768, married a rich wife, built himself a mansion in Saratoga, and made a fortune outfitting the rebel armies. As had Gouverneur Morris, Duer served in New York's provincial congress and the Continental Congress. In recognition of his financial wizardry, he was made Secretary of the Treasury Board in 1786, and three years later, Alexander Hamilton appointed him Assistant Secretary of the Treasury.

What Barlow lacked in business experience (solely confined to a brief period in which he owned a store that sold rum and molasses) he made up in charm and enthusiasm. His letters to his wife Ruth, written during their constant separations, are among the epistolary gems of the period. Barlow, a native of Redding, Connecticut, had gone to Yale when its campus consisted of two small buildings and a chapel. As an undergraduate, he made friends with a tutor named Abraham Baldwin, the son of a Guilford blacksmith who had managed to send his three sons to Yale and on to distinguished careers—Dudley as a lawyer, Henry as an Associate Justice of the Supreme Court, and Abraham, the first Senator from Georgia. There was also a sister, Ruth. Joel fell in love with Ruth, but her father, the erstwhile blacksmith, thought his prospects too poor—"the rhyming lover," he called him contemptuously. So Joel and Ruth were secretly married, a bold move in Puritan New England, and kept it secret a full year.

Joel, John Trumbull, and Elisha Babcock had started the *American Mercury* in Hartford. (John Trumbull—no relation to the painter—passed his entrance exams for Yale at seven but decided to wait until he was thirteen to enter). Timothy Dwight, Dr. Lemuel Hopkins, and David Humphreys added their talents, and the group became known variously as the Connecticut Wits, the Hartford Wits, and the Wicked Wits. Their magnum opus was *The Anarchiad*, a political satire

21

which ran in *The Mercury* for a year and became one of the young republic's first best sellers.

When Brissot de Warville made his trip to America to study its revolutionary methods at first hand, he had become an ardent admirer of Hartford and its Wits. Now Brissot was one of the most powerful men in France—one reason, perhaps, that Barlow was selected to represent Scioto.

Barlow left Ruth with her brother in Connecticut and set off on a filthy, flea-ridden frigate to proselytize to the Old World the wonders of the New. On his arrival, Barlow found France in the throes of "a certain political ferment." At the same time, he warned his parents and friends in the United States against the false news disseminated by the British. To be sure, France was in a state of agitation, but contrary to British allegations, there had been no massacres. Moreover, Lafayette had not been arrested, as the British papers reported, but only deprived of his command. And true, "Colonel Armand" was locked up in the Bastille, but this in no way dampened Barlow's faith in the future. In his eyes, France was making great strides toward a constitutional monarchy that would please everybody.

# 2

So it was that at the beginning of 1789, Paris welcomed a new center of American influence: Joel Barlow opened his offices on the rue des Petits-Champs near the Palais Royal in the very center of the city. There, to anyone interested in breaking ground on the banks of the Scioto, he gave out information, showed maps, distributed prospectuses, and answered queries from the provinces.

As the French political situation grew more uncertain, the idea of emigration began to take hold, and America seemed an ideal destination. People had been disappointed too often: first, they had placed their hopes on Calonne and his financial sleights of hand, then for a moment it had seemed as if the Notables might bring forth a solution, and now confidence in the future of the kingdom was waning despite the calling of the States-General. Perhaps they would have better luck elsewhere.

As early as 1784, disillusionment with Louis XVI's reign had brought a few enterprising Frenchmen to Franklin's house to ask for help in facilitating their move to the United States. Franklin had tried to discourage what he thought of as ill-considered plans. To this end, he published "A Warning to Those Who Wish to Go to America."

> Whatever the government may have been able to do in the past, it may at present enter into no agreement to help any person establish himself in the United States, whether by paying his passage, or giving him land, negroes, tools, herds, or any kind of emolument. And finally, America is a land of workers and in no way what the French call a "land of plenty" where the streets are paved with loaves of bread, the houses covered with omelettes and where already roasted chickens fly about crying "Eat me!"

The tract furnished a realistic picture of conditions in a country "full of immense forests, and empty of inhabitants." But for all his efforts, Franklin was not able to discourage the dreamers, and when he left France, they turned to his successor.

Although the passage of time has destroyed most of their entreaties, Jefferson—a tidy man—kept in his files a letter from a thirty-three-year-old carpenter named Jacques Ragondez. Addressing Jefferson very politely as "Monseigneur," the supplicant spilled out his troubles: he was tired of working the land with his father "Paul Ragondez, laborer, beyond the Gobelin Gate"; he had tried carpentry, but this had worked out no better than agriculture, and he was now thinking about emigrating. "That is why I am taking the liberty of addressing myself to you, having heard that in the New World and specifically in the province of Pennsylvania, there are vast uncultivated lands only waiting for industrious men to come and cultivate them."

Determined to give up his job as foreman to "a master carpenter of the King and the Hôtel des Monnoyes in Paris and to go to the above-mentioned country," Ragondez entreated Jefferson to inform him of "the most advantageous and least costly way" to accomplish his purpose. Once he was there, what would be his rights and prerogatives? And how could he become an American citizen and "one of the supporters of the infant republic"?

Paris and the provinces filled Jefferson's mail with similar requests as the Scioto Company's enticing prospectuses hit their mark, and aristocrats were taken in along with bourgeois, artisans, and the commonest people.

The Marquise de Lafayette went out of her way to support her husband and extend every kindness to all Americans. She had the Misses Jefferson liberated from their convent to come visit her in the country. And if John Trumbull happened to be in Paris while the marquis was away, she devoted herself to making his stay as pleasant as possible. Soon after the opening of his Paris offices, Joel Barlow received an invitation to dine at the Hôtel de Lafayette, and as a gracious gesture to her American guest, the marquise had the invitation printed in English.

In fact, the marquise's entire family shared the same enthusiasm for the United States: her father, the Duc d'Ayen; her brother, the Vicomte de Noailles; but above all her aunt, the Comtesse de Tessé, the Duc d'Ayen's sister. The head of the family, old Maréchal de Noailles, and Mme. de Tessé had come by their love for America through their love of gardens. The maréchal coveted American seed and American plants for his fields at Saint-Germain-en-Laye, as did Mme. de Tessé for her English and Chinese flowerbeds in Chaville. Thus would the democratic sprouts which had germinated in the land of liberty raise their heads among the proud blossoms of the Noailles gardens. However, as everywhere else, politics was gaining on gardening. If Mme. de Tessé sighed over the delayed arrival of the seed Jefferson had ordered for her from Virginia, she was even more concerned for the kingdom's new constitution.

Jefferson heard the first rumblings and feared "some sort of explosion" if the King did not quickly adopt the measures advocated. The same men who had admired American freedoms now pleaded for reforms: Brissot, Condorcet, the La Rochefoucauld family, the veterans of the War of Independence, and a number of academicians, financiers and economists such as Ray de Chaumont, Du Pont de Nemours, and the Le Couteulx family.

The salons and cafés bubbled with ideas and swarmed with men eager to give advice and offer nostrums. Jefferson listened to the theorists and read the gazettes and leaflets to familiarize himself with the plans for the constitution, with the financial, fiscal, and legal reforms, as well as with the "considerations on the free circulation of seed" whose repercussions might well influence the exportation of American cereals.

The Club de Valois was one hub of intellectual ferment; its patron was the Duc d'Orléans. Jefferson was a member and often took William Short to its meetings in the Palais Royal, where it occupied two floors of an imposing building. There, one was likely to rub elbows with Lafayette, the Duc de Lauzun, the Vicomte de Noailles, all veterans of the American campaign; with the young Duc de Chartres, d'Ayen, La Rochefoucauld, de Liancourt, Condorcet, Talleyrand (then Bishop d'Autun); and with such foreigners as the Count of Dorset, the Prince of Salm, Baron de Staël (the son-in-law of Finance Minister Jacques Necker), Count

Fersen, Tronchin and Perrégaux from Switzerland, and even Gouverneur Morris.

During this period, Jefferson wrote to Madison: "Everybody here is trying their hands at forming declarations of rights. As something of that kind is going on with you also, I send you two specimens from hence." The demands were not unfamiliar to the Americans: suppression of arbitrary distinctions between the King's subjects, religious freedom, freedom of the press, *habeas corpus,* and a single property tax. The reformers started with the same assumptions: that all men were created equal, that their property rights must be assured as well as their liberty and honor, that all sovereignty resided essentially in the state, that taxes should be levied with the consent of the taxed, and that no one should be molested for his opinions or his faith.

Reform was on everyone's mind, but the country was insatiable: it always wanted more. Jefferson found himself at loggerheads with Lafayette, who, sweeping diplomatic niceties aside, kept urging Jefferson to take a hand in shaping a declaration for the French people as he had for the Americans. The United States minister bridled at this proposition; he respected the restraints imposed by his functions, and he was embarrassed at the idea of suggesting a line of conduct for France. He was on firm ground where his own country was concerned, where the hopes of the future had taken precedence over the realities of the past, but he was much less sure of himself when dealing with the Kingdom of France bent under the weight of its ancient traditions. In the course of their conversations, Jefferson intimated that he feared the opening of the floodgates and the French people's impulsive temperament. Better gradually to ameliorate the people's condition with the aim of achieving a monarchic regime tempered by a parliament. A compromise between the nobility and the Third Estate was essential; otherwise the King was left with only one alternative: to opt for the Third Estate, the backbone of the country, and govern with it to the exclusion of everyone else. If, however, things were properly organized, Louis XVI could be solidly ensconced on his throne, with Lafayette in his ministry.

Wary though he was, Jefferson ended by giving in to his convictions. He secretly drew up a Proposition for a Charter Describing the Rights of the Sovereign and the Rights of the Nation. In this paper he recommended the abolition of privileges and suggested an annual meeting of the States-General as the only body qualified to vote laws and levy taxes. But he also accorded the King a generous civil list, concluding "better to buy liberty than make a revolution."

Locked in a drawer, the "Proposition" was shown to only the most privileged friends.

The Salle des Menus-Plaisirs at Versailles was being readied for the coming meeting of the States-General when Lafayette called one morning at the Hôtel de Langeac. Gouverneur Morris happened to be there as well and, being Morris, was struck by the informality of Lafayette's dress. Why had the marquis abandoned the proper ceremony?

The three men discussed the coming meetings at Versailles. Morris proposed that when the King opened the assembly he would do well to remove the foreign mercenaries and replace his Swiss Guard with French troops. His two interlocutors found the matter of little interest; they had quite different problems on their minds. Lafayette was concerned for his own position: as a deputy of the nobility, yet devoted to the people, he was torn between allegiance to the gentry and to the Third Estate. Should he show his hand and throw himself into the fray without further delay, or would he do better to sit by and await developments? He looked to Jefferson to pluck him from his uncertainty. Gouverneur Morris' presence did not embarrass him; he thought Morris could be trusted.

The two Americans advised him to be cautious. The marquis could always reveal his position when the time was ripe. Lafayette accepted their view without argument. He was glad to be governed by persons more experienced in politics than he, especially when they were Americans.

The inauguration of the States-General began on May 8, 1789, with a procession. As it filed toward the Church of Saint-Louis, Jefferson was shocked at the way the aristocratic pretensions of the prelates kept them separated from the simple priests. On the other hand, hopes soared as the Duc d'Orléans, La Rochefoucauld, de Liancourt, the Comte de Clermont-Tonnerre, Lafayette, and the Vicomte de Noailles took their places in the ranks of the nobility. When the veterans of the American war marched by, one man was notably absent: the Marquis de La Roüerie had been rejected as a delegate by the Breton nobility, for they did not trust him. Filled with bitterness, La Roüerie took to the woods with his friend Schaffner. From that time on, he railed against anything and everything done at Versailles and spoke out against every reform, taking the smallest liberal innovation as a personal affront.

Of the meeting itself, Jefferson wrote:

Viewing it as opera it was imposing; as a scene of business the king's speech was exactly what it should have been and very well delivered, not a word of the Chancellor's was heard by anybody, so that as yet I have never heard a single guess at what it was about. Mr. Necker's was as good as such a number of details would permit it to be. The picture of their resources was consoling & generally plausible. I could have wished him to have dwelt more on those great constitutional reformations which his *Rapport au roy* had prepared us to expect.

And he concluded: "The Noblesse . . . are not as much reformed in their principles as we had hoped they would be."

Jefferson's sympathies were stirred only when he saw the lowliest clergy associate themselves with the Third Estate. As for his friend Lafayette, his equivocal position led Jefferson to write George Washington:

> I am in great pain for the M. de Lafayette. His principles as you know are clearly with the people. But having been elected for the noblesse of Auvergne they have laid him under express instructions to vote for the decisions by orders and not persons. This would ruin him with the tiers-état . . . I have not hesitated to press on him to burn his instructions and follow his conscience as the only sure clue which will eternally guide a man clear of all doubts and inconsistencies.

Meanwhile, Lafayette was hard at work on his Declaration of the Rights of Man. America was implicit in the text, for the young republic was constantly in his mind. Before taking sides, Lafayette always asked himself: "What would the United States do in this situation?" And off he would go to consult Jefferson.

May and most of June passed, bringing with them their harvest of disillusion. The States-General were marking time. The three orders were unable to work together or reach an agreement, and concerned Americans like Jefferson and Morris were growing anxious. Jefferson suggested to Lafayette that, in order to allay the people's impatience, he organize a free distribution of bread. Morris, on the other hand, feared the eventual leveling of classes far more than he did famine. The egalitarian principle seemed to him "very problematical," and equality among Frenchmen struck him as pure folly. Jefferson simply smiled at Morris' hobgoblins.

Then came the day when the deputies found the doors to their meeting place closed by order of the King. Led by Mirabeau and Sieyès, the representatives of the Third Estate immediately gathered at the Jeu de Paume, and having three days earlier declared themselves a National Assembly, took a solemn oath to remain for as long as it would take to draft a constitution. That day, June 20, marked the beginning of the Revolution.

When the Fourth of July came around, Jefferson celebrated the anniversary of the Declaration of Independence with a luncheon at the Hôtel de Langeac, and William Short helped him with the honors. Short was just back from an extended tour of Italy (where he had delivered Jefferson's designs for mantelpieces for Monticello to a marbleworker in Genoa) and southern France (where he had bought several cases of wine for Jefferson's cellar). Among those present, Virginia was represented by John and Lucy Paradise, in Europe on a pleasure trip, and Jefferson's Monticello neighbor, Philip Mazzei. However, Yankees predominated, most of them based in Paris except for Thomas Appleton, down from Rouen, and Daniel Parker, a partner of William Duer, who had come over from London. Joel Barlow, whose wife was reluctant to cross the ocean, took advantage of his temporary celibacy to flirt with Mrs. Blackden. Morris, for once choosing politics over gallantry, remarked to Lafayette: "The current is getting so strong against the Noblesse that I apprehend their Destruction."

But Lafayette was not impressed with Morris' forebodings: he had other things on his mind. Two days later, he sent Jefferson the final draft of his Declaration of the Rights of Man with the request that the minister look it over, consider it, and return it with his observations. Jefferson wrote back: "I will bring you the paper you desire tomorrow and shall dine at the Dutchess Danville [*sic*] where I shall be happy to meet you."


While the United States minister and his guests were drinking to his country's independence, Mirabeau was thundering at Versailles. Shaking his powdered wig at the Assembly's Committee of Supplies, the orator suggested that Necker be put out to pasture. (He secretly coveted the gentleman's portfolio as Minister of Finance.) Then he went on to ask, not without impertinence, what fate the Cabinet had in mind for "the proposals to furnish provisions, made by M. Jefferson in America's name."

Malicious to the core, Mirabeau deliberately used this device to inflame public opinion because it involved the population's essential food, bread. The subject of hunger was on everyone's lips, even at the tables of the rich where guests castigated Necker and reduced his politics to crumbs—along with the *pâté en croûte.*

The proposal Mirabeau was referring to had been offered the preceding year by James Swan and Samuel Blackden.

Already concerned with the scarcity of bread, they suggested replenishing France's supply with American cereals and grains. The two men had gone to the Hôtel de Ville to discuss the matter with the King's attorney, Ethis de Corny, a friend of America and veteran of the War of Independence. Unfortunately, the problem did not lie within his jurisdiction: only Necker was qualified to deal with such an offer. Usually, de Corny communicated with Necker through the minister's chief clerk, Tarbé. De Corny offered to give Tarbé the dossier the Americans had brought, lending it the full weight of his authority. Swan and Blackden accepted the proposition gladly and subsequently satisfied themselves that the dossier had indeed reached Necker. From that moment on, they never stopped for breath. They redoubled their efforts, even going so far as to inform Necker that they were prepared to go to the United States to bring back grains and flour. If payment was a complicating factor—France's finances being in a delicate state—Swan and Blackden would accept payment in French manufactured products. Thus the country would reap a double benefit. But for all their zeal, Necker would not budge. So they asked Lafayette to track down their dossier, first reminding him that since many countries did not permit the exportation of cereals, the United States was France's most accessible granary. But Lafayette's voice also fell on deaf ears. Then the financier Le Couteulx was asked to intercede; he suggested to Necker that France tie the repayment of the American debt to the offer of grain, but he too got no response. At the year's end, Swan addressed an ultimatum to Tarbé, but his letter vanished.

And now Mirabeau was exhuming this stillborn child to frighten the government and attaching Jefferson's name to it to give it greater weight.

Thus implicated, Jefferson was forced to reply and state the truth. He protested that he had never made the slightest overture to the Finance Minister about importing wheat; all he had done, and at Necker's behest, was to inform his government of the urgent need that threatened France. American newspapers had published his letter to prod native merchants into making offers to France. His role had gone no further.

Debate shifted to the committee entrusted with drafting a constitution. Once again, Jefferson was unwillingly drawn into the conflict. The question dividing the committee centered on the monarch's veto, with the partisans of the absolute veto ranged against those who wanted none. When the battle threatened to reach an impasse, Lafayette decided that only private conversations could resolve the conflict. And since a meeting at his *hôtel* was impossible—the house was being watched and word might leak out through his servants—he thought to have his colleagues meet at the Hôtel de Langeac. He wrote Jefferson from Versailles, asking him to cancel all engagements for the following day and prepare a luncheon for eight members of the Assembly to whom the invitation had already been issued. The seriousness of the situation justified his boldness; in fact, he explained, if the question of the veto was not immediately resolved, the dissolution of the Assembly and even civil war might well follow. There was nothing left but for Jefferson to summon his *maître d'hôtel* and order the meal.

The guests who made their appearance on rue Neuve-de-Berry the next day included Lafayette, Theodore Lameth (a veteran of the War of Independence), Adrien Duport, Barnave, the Marquis de Blacons, the Marquis de Latour-Maubourg, the Comte d'Agoult, and finally, Jean-Joseph

Mounier, the most prominent of the monarchists, who wanted to see the sovereign buttressed by two chambers, as in England.

Jefferson welcomed his guests with his usual grace, and after a few polite exchanges, invited them into the dining room. Once the table was cleared and the wines brought in (an American custom borrowed from the British), the servants retired. By now it was four o'clock. Lafayette led off, explaining the reasons for the clandestine gathering: the problem of the veto must be resolved in private in order to bind the deputies present into a solid bloc. By their unanimity they could guarantee a general decision that would allow the King to postpone execution of laws—a suspensive veto—but not kill them outright.

Jefferson saw to the wines while avoiding any direct participation in the discussion, which lasted until ten o'clock that night. He remained mute and did not so much as blink an eye, even though he later described the discussion as "worthy of being placed in parallel with the finest dialogue of antiquity, as handed to us by Xenophon, by Plato, and Cicero." Lafayette had placed him in an untenable position: against his will, he had been asked to use the legation to camouflage a gathering of conspirators. The King, to whom he was accredited, would have every reason to take offense, for this meeting was bound to become an open secret. With Lafayette's horses champing outside the Hôtel de Langeac, his men chatting with Jefferson's Swiss guard, possibly even with passersby, the police and their spies would have every reason to suspect the worst.

So, losing no time, Jefferson presented himself to the Foreign Minister the very next day. Montmorin had already been informed but he was grateful for the American's gesture—which did not surprise him, for he knew Jefferson to be a gentleman.

Unlike Jefferson, Joel Barlow, or William Short, Gouverneur Morris was interested neither in France's convulsions nor in the cause of liberty and equality. Morris felt the same distaste for men of ideas as he did for the common people, and the marriage of these two groups filled him with disgust. But his predilection for the powerful did not prevent him from seeing things clearly, so he condemned abuses when the occasion demanded it, though always preaching moderation and a repudiation of all "systems." In any event, his tastes ran to the Epicurean, and the amorous aspects of Paris attracted him far more than reforms.

(In America, where risque stories were frowned upon, everyone had accepted his version of how he had lost his leg—a story involving a frightened horse, an overturned carriage, and an unfortunate wheel that had crushed his leg. But a much different version circulated around the Chaussée d'Antin and the Faubourg Saint-Germain: there it was said that Morris had been fleeing a husband and shattered his leg when he jumped from his beloved's window.)

Soon after his arrival in Paris, Morris' covetous eye fell on the Comtesse de Flahaut, and she in turn delighted in his company. Adélaïde de Flahaut was already Talleyrand's "official mistress," and as the bishop had a clubfoot, it occurred to her that it might be amusing to add a second cripple to her conquests.

When Louis XV had grown old, ladies of easy virtue let it be known that they owed their existence to capers of the well-beloved king. John Paul Jones reported that an adventuress named Mme. Townsend, persuaded she was a bastard of the gallant king, would occasionally disappear, pretending she was going to Versailles to visit her half-sisters, Mme. Adélaïde and Mme. Victoire.

Mme. de Flahaut made no pretense of royal origin, for her family's history was too well known. She was the natural daughter of Bouret, the *Fermier-Général,* and her mother was a member of the lesser provincial nobility who had married beneath her—a local wine distributor named Filleul—in order to legitimize her oldest daughter, supposedly the child of a union with Louis XV. M. Filleul was nothing if not accommodating and permitted his wife to become Bouret's mistress openly. At the same time, she cultivated the Poisson family. There she found a husband for her first-born, who, by marrying the Marquis de Marigny, became Mme. de Pompadour's sister-in-law.

Mme. Filleul died before she had time to provide for her younger daughter, who was reduced to marrying an older man, the Comte de Flahaut. His only fortune rested in a brother, the Marquis d'Angiviller, manager of the King's buildings. The marquis's influence assured his brother a sinecure and rooms in the Louvre, which at that time was encumbered with such parasites.

Soon after his arrival in Paris, Gouverneur Morris started visiting the spirited Adélaïde in the old palace, at the same time picking up tips on the manners of French aristocracy. He often crossed paths with the Bishop d'Autun, carrying a bed-warmer destined for a bed that Morris hoped to occupy in turn.

In anticipation, the American embarked on his apprenticeship in Paris mores. He soon learned to copy the daily rounds of the nobility: a morning of work with his secretary, sometimes interrupted by a caller, then visits to various titled ladies (who were often out calling on each other), meetings with this minister or that, then dinner at one or another *hôtel,* and sometimes at a *traiteur,* forerunner of the restaurant. And as Mme. de Flahaut began to weave her seductive web, he spent more and more time at her apartments in the Louvre.

Sometimes she would plead illness when he came to visit. In mid-June, exasperation drove Morris to write in his diary: "She has three formidable enemies: herself, her Sickness but above all her Doctor who together are going to give her a terrible time." Her fall, though she had no way of foreseeing it, coincided with the fall of the Bastille.

As Morris made his daily calls, he noticed the growing tension in the streets of Paris. On July 12, as he was crossing the Place Louis XV (later renamed place de la Concorde), he saw a crowd of about a hundred people throwing stones at a group of cavalrymen with drawn sabers. After a brief skirmish, the cavalry found it prudent to ride off.

On July 14, sick with fever and with a cold coming on, Morris went to see Le Couteulx on business. Someone rushed in to announce the fall of the Bastille: the governor and the *provost des marchands* had been beheaded "and their heads carried in Triumph through the City." The informant added that the mob had broken into Les Invalides and had arms enough for an army of thirty thousand.*

---

* For three days, wild disorder had spread through the streets of Paris, a reaction, in part, to the movement of royal troops to the city and Versailles, and in part, to the King's dismissal of Necker. The July 14 attack on the Bastille, the first serious violence in the Revolution, marked a new phase as the people of Paris toppled the King's representatives and elected their own local government—the Commune. Louis XVI was forced to recall Necker, recognize the newly elected government of the city, and confirm Lafayette as head of the National Guard. The King himself then donned the revolutionary tricolor cockade.

Morris rushed to the Louvre to inform Mme. de Flahaut. They were turning to more intimate topics when her husband arrived. In a spirit of deviltry, Morris dashed off a few verses in English, knowing that only Adélaïde understood the language. When the Comte de Flahaut asked for a translation, he was not at all amused to find that he was referred to as "too old to raise in you a mutual Flame."

By July 20, Morris' patience was at an end. His entry in his diary reports: "Give her some verses and with infinite Coolness and Seriousness tell her that I cannot consent to be only her Friend. . . ." The next day, since Paris was talking of little else, Morris procured two passes to take Adélaïde to the Bastille. She shivered with revulsion as the infatuated Morris guided her through the dark dungeons. He remarked only that "it stank horribly."

Two days later, Morris quotes her response to his confession: ". . . to cure me of the Passion, she avows a Marriage of the Heart. I guess the Person. She acknowledges it and assures me that she cannot commit an Infidelity to him." But he adds: "By degrees however we come very near it."

On July 27, Morris records: "Madame is at her toilet. Mons. [the count] comes in. . . . Monsieur leaves us to make a long Visit and we are to occupy ourselves with making a translation. We sit down with the best Disposition imaginable but instead of a translation. . . ." Thus did Adélaïde's capitulation follow on the heels of the Bastille's, and Morris duly noted the victory in his journal. A man of punctilious habits, he kept a strict accounting of his every fall from grace.

Months later, Morris could write: "She is still apprehensive of the Consequences. If, however, nothing happens, we are to take care for the future until the Husband returns, and then exert ourselves to add one to the Number of human Existences."

If the fall of the Bastille meant less to Morris than that of Mme. de Flahaut, to Lafayette, the event was a symbol: it represented the key to a fortress violated by the people in the name of liberty, a key he intended to send as homage to George Washington.

To the painter Trumbull, the Bastille was a deserving subject. Pad and pencil in hand, he rushed over from London, made sketches, listened, reflected, and wrote to his brother: "I conceived that the taking of the Bastille and the King's visit to Paris were proper subjects to painting. I found them so. I have gratified my curiosity, secured such materials as will enable me to paint the two subjects hereafter and returned to London yesterday."

In May the calling of the States-General, in June the oath of the Jeu de Paume, in July the storming of the Bastille. Each month had brought with it its tableaux and memorable words. The night of August 4 proved that France was not finished with surprises. The enthusiasm kindled by the abolition of privileges had not yet subsided when the Assembly adopted the Declaration of the Rights of Man, as proposed by Lafayette and discreetly reviewed by Jefferson.

Meanwhile public opinion was paying little heed to the cracks beginning to show in the walls of their temple to constitutional monarchy. The Marquis de La Roüerie had sharper eyes than most of his contemporaries and was one of the first to discern the fissures in the new edifice. Perhaps his bitterness at having been excluded helped open his eyes. Whatever the reason, he sensed the approaching struggle, and like the Comte d'Artois, the King's brother, condemned all reforms, the good with the bad. But whereas the comte had emigrated to Coblenz and become the center of royalist forces on foreign soil, La Roüerie disapproved of such a step. For him, the battle would be fought on native soil: those loyal to the King should close ranks around him rather than lead lives of ease beyond the nation's frontiers and among the King's traditional enemies.

The faithful Schaffner was easily made to share these views and helped La Roüerie polish his armor. It was a strange destiny indeed that was leading this Protestant commoner to draw his sword in the defense of an aristocracy tightly bound to the outward symbols of Catholicism and its privileges.

So, separated from their former companions-at-arms, La Roüerie and Schaffner applauded neither the capture of the Bastille (despite the marquis's unpleasant memories of that prison), nor the oath of the Jeu de Paume, and even less the events of the night of August 4.

Jefferson received permission from his government to spend the winter in America and took his daughters with him. He would return with the first swallows in 1790. During his absence, William Short was to continue the legation's work and everything at the Hôtel de Langeac would proceed as usual under M. Petit's watchful eye.

Jefferson took advantage of the trip to take back several pictures and busts, a harpsichord, and a few bibelots for Monticello. He also took a gig and a phaeton for his personal use, as well as cases of wine (Sauterne, Frontignan, Rochegude, and Montrachet), cartons of groceries, and a full complement of kitchen utensils picked out by Jim, an authority on such matters. His American friends had swamped him with requests, among them books for Benjamin

Franklin and two busts of John Paul Jones, one destined for John Jay. And last but not least, his passion for gardening led him to bring sacks of seed and cases of roots and plants, promising a harvest of melons, figs, strawberries, roses, pistachios, and mimosa. In the hold, pine, oak, and locust nestled next to heather and ivy. He even included Crassane pears.

All these flowers, shrubs, and fruits were so many garlands to friendship—or perhaps wreaths for the tombs of lost hopes. In fact, as he was preparing to leave all his half-finished projects and the many friends already awaiting his return, Jefferson learned that he had been appointed Secretary of State. His new post would keep him in America, and he was leaving France for good.

# 3

The October days* followed on the heels of Jefferson's departure. The procession of women led by Théroigne de Méricourt in her cocked hat, and the National Guard with Lafayette on his white horse in the lead, passed the Chaillot Gate, took the road to Versailles, and returned with the royal family. The Hôtel de Langeac furnished an ideal observation post for the procession in both directions.

Although William Short did not communicate his personal impressions to Jefferson, he did send him newspapers and kept him abreast of the American colony's activities. Daniel Parker, Colonel Swan, and Gouverneur Morris were badgering Necker and Montmorin with proposals on imports. Determined to succeed where the others had failed, Morris was offering Necker the Hudson Valley's harvest, and

* On October 1, 1789, a lavish dinner was given at Versailles in honor of the arriving royal troops called in by the King from their garrisons in Flanders. To a starving populace in Paris, the dinner was a double insult—food was being lavished on unwanted troops. October 5 saw a "bread march" of poor Parisians on Versailles. Only the arrival of Lafayette and the National Guard prevented a bloodbath as the marchers reached the royal troops ringed around Versailles. Lafayette dismissed the royal guard and moved to protect the royal family. Gangs of rioters still

following Swan and Blackden's initiative, he tied the payment for its cereals to the American debt. It was decided that Amsterdam would be the most convenient place to carry out the transaction.

The question of the debt to France had gone through many permutations since the days when the first loans had been granted by the Court of Versailles at Beaumarchais's prompting. In 1788, Etienne Clavière, Mirabeau's friend and Necker's foe, had tried, with Brissot's help, to refinance the debt, but it had come to nothing. As the two countries became equally hard pressed, they laboriously worked out various arrangements, but to achieve its ends, America was forced to seek loans from Dutch bankers. Beginning in 1790, a little money started to trickle into the French treasury.

In his letters to Jefferson, Short shuttled between business matters and those relating to the Hôtel de Langeac. The carriage horses were well, although—sad to relate—one saddle horse had developed a limp that refused to get well. "I have had him put in the petites affiches & took other measures for disposing of him, but the market is so glutted that it will be very difficult to dispose of him on any terms."

His pen took wing as he reported the news that a sequel to Jean-Jacques Rousseau's *Confessions* had just appeared in the bookshops, and the literary crowd and salon gossips were pouncing on the volume "with unexampled avidity." Most of

---

managed to break into the palace and kill several of the Queen's bodyguards. The next morning, October 6, the King bowed to the mob and agreed to follow it back to Paris. En route, the shout was heard: "We have the Baker and the Baker's Wife and the little Baker's boy—now we shall have bread." The royal family never returned to Versailles. They were installed in the palace of the Tuileries, virtual prisoners. The national Assembly soon followed, abandoning Versailles for Paris, the King for the people. In the same month, the King authorized a National Constituent Assembly to create a constitution.

its readers were looking only for scandal, for in it, Jean-Jacques made no bones of his passion for the Marquise d'Houdetot, nor did he attempt to hide the lady's liaison with Saint-Lambert. Short was unable to tell Jefferson how Rousseau's heroine was taking it, for he had had no occasion to see her since the bombshell burst. He assumed that most women would be delighted to see themselves "represented in such flattering colors." On the other hand, "poor Grimm," a frequent guest at the Hôtel de Langeac, was described by Rousseau as a despicable schemer. Baron Grimm had taken to his bed and refused all visitors, including Short.

Mme. de Corny added her own embellishments in her letter to Jefferson: "Rousseau's portrait of [Mme. d'Houde-tot] is not a likeness at all, and I defy you to recognize her, so carefully has he removed her squint."

What an autumn harvest! The salons hummed with literature and malice. Mme. de Corny made a casual reference to Parisian society's dispersal and the difficulty that men of breeding were encountering in finding posts, and added as an afterthought: "We are having a terrible shortage of bread."

So the earth continued to turn in spite of the Revolution. If in July the head of the governor of the Bastille had been impaled on a pike, and in October the Queen had fled her bedroom in her underwear, stockings in hand, Jefferson's grooms still curried the horses, the *Petites Affiches* continued to titillate the public, the Americans went on about their business, the Condorcets' salon kept on spinning gilded encomiums to the New France, and the Faubourg Saint-Germain delighted in Rousseau's cynical indiscretions.

The year was coming to an end with no solution to the monarchy's problems in sight. The installation of the

"Baker," the "Baker's Wife," and the little "Baker's boy" in the Tuileries did nothing to assuage the general misery. Bread was still lacking and the deficit would not go away. Many a lover of liberty despaired at the continuing malaise, and rather than wait for a solution, left for America and the promise of a less precarious life. Instead of the petulant emigration of men like the Comte d'Artois and the Prince de Condé, these wiser heads looked to a happy future in the New World. This played nicely into Joel Barlow's schemes, and the Scioto Company ship sailed on revolutionary tides, the wind in its sails.

Joel now had an associate, a respected English economist named William Playfair. Playfair helped him organize the French end of the enterprise and induced a prominent group of men to serve on its board of directors, including the Marquis de Lezay-Marnésia, Lally-Tollendal, Mounier, Malouet, and Duval d'Eprémesnil.

Once organized, the French Scioto Company published a prospectus for "those desiring to live in America." It was soon followed by a supplement to keep public interest high; to embellish the text, Barlow instructed P. F. Tardieu to make an engraving of the territories bathed by the Ohio and Scioto rivers.

Soon another brochure appeared, describing the soil and its potential, and praising the fertile lands and waterways to be found between Pennsylvania and Lake Erie. It extolled the limpid Scioto, its banks thick with timber, where maples gushed a sweet liquid when scored with a knife. The yield of wheat and corn was better than any in Europe, and its tobacco—regardless of what Jefferson said—was superior to Virginia's. Whereas Franklin had gone to great lengths to counsel wisdom to the emigrants, Joel Barlow, William Playfair, and their French colleague, M. Boulogne, seemed to take delight in undermining his moderation. Their descriptions were music to French ears, and clients came flocking.

In four months the Scioto Company sold five hundred tracts, and five hundred buyers paid the asking price, although the motley crowd of wigmakers, jewelers, cooks, gilders, carriage makers, and music masters seemed an unlikely lot to be taming the virgin forest.

Riding the crest of euphoria, Joel Barlow expressed his optimism in a letter to William Duer, the organizer of the New York branch of the Scioto Company: business was marvelous and clients were beating on his door in ever increasing numbers. Barlow had also begun negotiations with the Royal Treasury for the liquidation of depreciated American bonds that were needlessly cluttering up His Majesty's coffers. Barlow offered land in exchange for the bonds. To demonstrate the extent of his confidence, he authorized Duer to take out a loan of one hundred thousand francs, to be followed by another of the same amount in ninety days. He anticipated an immediate profit of at least one million francs.

To his beloved wife in her New England solitude, Joel described his clients in more flattering terms: the kitchen helpers and wigmakers became rich and titled personages, and even included a few members of the Assembly. Paris had only to hear the first reports from the happy settlers, he told Ruth, and a million new emigrants would soon follow.

Only one element was missing to complete his happiness: he did not have a single official document, not one deed that guaranteed the Scioto Company rights to the territories in question. He pleaded with Duer to bring the matter before Congress. Duer failed to answer his appeals, and for many months Paris had no news from New York. Left to his own devices, Barlow forged ahead, even as his distinguished board of directors fell by the wayside, victim of the political uncertainties.

The revolutionary seesaw was plummeting some to the depths while others rose to the summit. One victim was Mounier, who had played an important role during the October Days, then retired from public life to live in the provinces. Duval d'Eprémesnil, after riding high on the first revolutionary wave, was soon abandoned by all his following. Just as the Marquis de La Roüerie had moved against the government in 1787 in the hope that Louis XVI's humiliation might serve the cause of Breton liberties, d'Eprémesnil had raised the standard of revolt to help the parliamentarians triumph over the King. When each discovered that the Revolution favored neither provincial autonomy nor the parliamentary forces, they quickly retreated from the liberty they had so recently worshiped. Both men sought refuge in the shadow of the throne—a lesser evil in their eyes. Banking his ardor for the time being, d'Eprémesnil thought America might prove his salvation, or his last hope if the situation worsened. As one of the first revolutionaries, one of those who had called the States-General, he could hardly turn eastward and join the princes in Germany. So he looked west to the United States and bought more than ten thousand acres of Scioto land.

As for the Marquis de Lezay-Marnésia, philanthropic zeal had once moved him to abolish all forced labor on his estates, and he had been one of the first to break with the nobility in the States-General and join the Third Estate. But he too was beginning to have second thoughts. Was France really about to enter a golden age? If human baseness was going to prevail over liberalism, well then, he would go elsewhere to set up the republic of his dreams—and he had the means to do so.

So he picked up stakes and prepared to leave for Scioto. One of his sons left the army to join him, and he recruited some of his best peasants and laborers by painting a glowing picture of the better world across the sea. A devout Catholic despite his revolutionary principles, the marquis demanded that each man furnish proof of confession before he enlisted; he even inveigled a Benedictine monk to accompany him by obtaining a papal bull that elevated him to the episcopate, as the first Bishop of Scioto. The monk absconded with several precious vases and liturgical ornaments from the Cathedral of Saint-Denis. Given the times and the risk to church property, he thought it an act of piety to transfer these treasures to the Cathedral of Scioto, a building in the clouds.

As the year 1789 came to an end, Joel Barlow sent M. Boulogne to Le Havre, where the first group of six hundred emigrants was making ready for a January departure. Boulogne supervised the outfitting of the ship and prepared to accompany the first convoy, while Joel stayed in Paris, following the pioneers in his thoughts. He wrote to Boulogne: "My heart goes with them. I consider them the fathers and founders of a nation." Onward to New France!

Neither Duer's silence nor Ruth's lamentations—she continued to bemoan her solitude while refusing to leave America—could dampen Barlow's enthusiasm. However, the new year soon brought its disappointments. The flow of money started to dwindle, and Barlow was obliged to ask for an advance from the bank of Debarth, Coquet et Cie. to cover his expenses.


With Jefferson's departure, William Short was left to his own devices, and as his self-confidence grew, so did his position in society. For several months his attachment to the daughter of the house in Saint-Germain had satisfied all his youthful ardor; he never would have dared cast his eyes on a duchess. But during the first winter on his own, his glance chanced to fall on the young Duchesse de La Rochefoucauld.

The Ancien Régime was not intolerant of certain family arrangements: in this case, Alexandrine Charlotte de Rohan-Chabot, familiarly known as Rosalie, had married her mother's brother, which made her both granddaughter and daughter-in-law of the Duchesse d'Anville. That admirable woman, who had brought Rosalie up, had been a friend of Voltaire and Turgot. Rosalie's husband, a duke and peer of the realm, widower and twice her age, was a learned man, well traveled, spoke several languages, and was a member of the Académie des Sciences. Open to new ideas, even to giving the franchise to the Negroes in the West Indies, La Roche-foucauld was an admirer of Franklin and had both translated and published the United States Constitution. Like his cousin the Duc de Liancourt, and Lafayette and Condorcet, he was a committed pro-American and shared their views.

The young duchess tried hard to raise herself to the intellectual level of her husband and grandmother. She readily adopted the opinions of her circle, be it on Necker, Mirabeau, the deficit, the most desirable constitution, or the rights of man. William Short was hardly older than she and still retained some of the awkwardness of youth; as a good Virginian, he loved nature, and Rosalie on her side adored the country, particularly the green hills of La Roche-Guyon where the family château stood high above the Seine. As they talked, they discovered they shared the same taste in books, the theater, and opera, and of all the writers, they both liked Rousseau best. As members of the Assembly, academicians, and ambassadors—those commonly seen at the Hôtel de La

Rochefoucauld—argued around them, the young American and the duchess exchanged observations that grew increasingly intimate with time. After one tête-à-tête, Rosalie wrote him a note in which she confessed: "It was very painful for me the other day to have to go to my grandmother's immediately after having left you. I had to collect myself and regain my composure. Fortunately the lack of light, which I took care to avoid by standing with my back to it, served to protect me from the glances of the curious and indifferent."

Thomas Jefferson had been Secretary of State for several weeks before the news of his nomination reached Europe. His elevation provided a frequent subject of conversation at the Société de 1789, a club founded at the end of the year to replace the Club de Valois. Brissot, Le Couteulx, Mirabeau, Sieyès, Lavoisier, the painter David, and the poet André Chénier—back from London to celebrate "The Oath of the Jeu de Paume" in verse—were all members. William Short had joined immediately, together with several other Americans, including Benjamin Franklin's grandson, Temple.

Jefferson's departure left Short in a quandary. Because of America's involvement in its first presidential elections, he had not yet been officially named chargé d'affaires. Was his diplomatic career in jeopardy? During his recent trip to Italy, he had given his prospects some thought and conveyed his concern in letters to Jefferson in Paris. Should he stay in Europe, or would it be wise to return to the United States? Weighing the pros and cons, his mentor came to the conclusion that "to pass the first half of your life in Europe and the latter in America is still worse. The attachments and habits formed here in your youth would render the evening of life more miserable still in America." Jefferson was certain that a brilliant career awaited him in his own country, especially if he first prepared for the bar. Then, his own emotions breaking through, he added: "I say it with a bleeding heart: for nothing can be more dreary than my situation will be when you and my daughters shall have left me. I look forward to it with dismay." A year later, with Jefferson gone and Short's appointment still uncertain, the new Secretary of State wrote to suggest that he come home and take Grayson's place in the Senate.

Word finally came that Short was indeed chargé d'affaires. Pleased though he was by the appointment, he began to eye the still vacant post of minister plenipotentiary—an interest shared by Rosalie, who was equally eager to see him remain in Paris.

The new chargé d'affaires carried out his government's instructions to the letter and prepared his reports to Philadelphia with the greatest care, basing his observations on a careful sounding of public opinion as it was reflected in the newspapers, the clubs, the ministries, and the salons. He also continued the negotiations on America's debt and the replenishment of its capital. The situation with regard to tobacco was a constant source of worry, for the laws that hindered its importation played into powerful interests on both sides of the Atlantic, involving even deputies in intrigues. Short decided he should have an observer at the Assembly to keep him abreast of political developments, particularly anything that concerned American interests. He consulted Lafayette, who recommended a remarkable little Alsatian named Ramond, ideally endowed to serve as America's ear at the Assembly, and discreetly attached him to the American legation.

The plight of the American sailors held captive in Algiers

was still unresolved. Before leaving Paris, Jefferson had left orders with the Dutch bankers to advance the necessary funds to ransom the sailors. He introduced Short to Father Chauvier of the Mathurins with these words: "He will remain at his post and will be able to handle any financial arrangements you are kind enough to contract for us."

Short had meanwhile received appeals for help from his despairing countrymen through a group of compassionate sailors whose ship had called at Algiers. Captain Richard O'Bryen, the spokesman for the unfortunate captives, wrote him secretly to describe his companions' suffering. Although they had miraculously escaped the plague, Algiers was a "damned city," and to his signature he appended "at present a captive slave."

As ill luck would have it, the National Assembly abolished all religious orders in February, the King approved the measure, the Mathurins ceased their activities, and with them vanished all hope for the sailors' release. Short, now helpless to save them, shared Jefferson's conviction that the United States might have to use force to bring the pirates to heel.

Ever since July 14, the new ideas had been attracting a growing number of partisans. The revolutionary comet had in particular drawn a number of British stars into its trail, all eager to watch the demolition of that symbol of despotism, the Bastille. William Wordsworth even crossed the Channel to visit the promised land. In Britain itself, statesmen like Charles Fox and even his opponent in Parliament, William Pitt, smiled on the young Revolution. And Sheridan's ardent love of France swept beyond the walls of Westminster to engulf the masses.

The scientist Joseph Priestley looked up from his test tubes long enough to declare himself in favor of the new ideas. He was soon followed by a chorus of poets, among them the Scotsman Robert Burns, who called down a divine curse on anyone attempting to snuff out the spark of liberty on the banks of the Seine. When the Bastille fell, Samuel Coleridge heard "the beating of humanity's heart," Robert Southey imagined that Rousseau's dream was about to come true, and a prophetic flame grazed the visionary William Blake.

Thomas Paine abandoned London for Paris to fill his lungs with the pure air of liberty. As the impassioned apostle of American independence, he was well known in France, and his writings had appeared in French translations. During the months he spent in Paris, he dined regularly with Lafayette, with Condorcet, at the Hôtel de La Rochefoucauld, as well as at Brissot's more modest quarters—all of them places where he could speak English. With winter over, he made preparations for his return to England and eventually the United States. On Paine's departure, Lafayette entrusted him with the key to the Bastille so that he might present it as a tribute to General Washington.

Benjamin West, the historical painter, was particularly moved by that key, which he saw when Paine arrived back in England en route to America. A Pennsylvania Quaker who had moved to London after studying in Rome, he remained a staunch American and republican even though he was court painter to George III. He was already infected with the symptoms of Romanticism, and the thought charmed him that this emblem of tyranny was to be placed in the hands of the man who had broken the bonds in America. Carried away with enthusiasm, he sketched a picture of the solemn moment as he imagined it, promising himself that he would one day commit it to canvas for the edification of future generations.

The Scioto Company continued to furnish journalists and pamphleteers with lively material: "The Dream of an Inhabitant of the Scioto, Published by Himself," "Letters of M. de V. in Answer to Observations Published by the Scioto Company," and "The Parliament of Paris Established on the Scioto" were among their literary attacks. Joel Barlow fought against these slurs with the ardor of a knight-errant protecting his beloved.

Not all the attacks were so easy to refute. Citizen Roux, a sergeant-major and member of the civil and military committee for the district of Prémont, wrote a pamphlet entitled "The New Mississippi, or the Dangers of Living on the Banks of the Scioto." In it, he warned the public against this "grave of emigrants" that swallowed up fortunes. Exposing the lies aimed at the public, on philosophical and political grounds, the author maintained that America's soil was barren, "a kind of whitish, dried up sand" whose moonlike aridity made it impossible for plants to take root. Trees were without taproots and remained standing thanks only to "a hairy growth that spread over the surface of the soil, nourishing itself on three to four inches of productive earth." The water was undrinkable, causing addiction to rum and tafia and, even worse, an excessive consumption of tea. These deplorable conditions carried Americans to their graves well before the age of forty-five, and their wives were unable to procreate after thirty. "Frenchmen," he concluded, "happiness lies in your own country; a man who runs about the world rarely becomes a man of substance."

Deaf to this advice, the Marquis de Lezay-Marnésia

hurried his departure. With his ship, laborers, and bishop all ready to go, he wandered the Paris streets arranging the minutest details of his future establishment.

Word finally came from Duer, but it was far from comforting: there was no answer to Barlow's urgent questions, but instead, a request for a loan of a hundred thousand francs. The Scioto Company was in serious straits, and the news was beginning to get about. But that was not all: the first letters from the emigrants who had sailed in January were reaching Paris, and they spelled disaster. The French had learned on arrival that their lands had never been released by the federal government, that Duer, the kingpin of the operation, had never held more than a simple option, and that he had Barlow selling lots for which the Scioto Company had no valid title.

At first the exiles had been completely disheartened. Then, making the best of a bad situation, a few held on to their dreams and appealed to the American government to find them land. The rest lost all appetite for the pioneering venture and sought a quick return to France by any means available, resigned to the abuses they had suffered under the Ancien Régime and the dangers of the present disorder.

Among the deserters was a young workman named Dallemagne who turned up in Paris during the month of July. With the help of a local printer he published a far more convincing warning than that of Citizen Roux. He called his tract "News of Scioto, or a Faithful Report on the Voyage and Misfortunes of a Parisian Recently Returned from That Country Where He Had Gone to Establish Himself."

The text opened in the patriotic mode: "Vive la France et Paris!" Then he proceeded to ask why in God's name there was this infatuation with the Scioto. The young Dallemagne attributed it to people fleeing their creditors, ambitious men seeking their fortune, and the naïveté of workmen and laborers "frivolous and unreliable, and avid for novelty"— like himself. He and eight of his neighbors had been taken in; they had sailed together, suffering through the entire crossing, sleeping on bare wood, nourished on salt foods and old biscuits, but always sustained by hope.

Their eyes were opened when they found themselves in Alexandria, a thousand miles from their destination, with only their miserable duffel bags and no means of existence.

Things looked bleak in the Paris headquarters of Scioto on the rue des Petits-Champs. The indignation of the families of the first group, and the wrath of the second then forming, took such a disquieting turn that Barlow and his staff no longer dared set foot in their offices. There were threats of assassination, and at a time when the mob considered street lights handy gallows, Barlow feared for his life. He left his furnished rooms and sought refuge with a compatriot, kicking himself for having been taken in by the Scioto mirage.

Benjamin Franklin's popularity had remained high from the day Louis XVI's subjects besieged his *hôtel* on learning that liberty's torch-bearer had arrived in Paris. One after the other, Houdon, Caffieri, Dupré, Greuze, Vanloo, and Duplessis reproduced his features in marble and on canvas, and his engraved portraits, after the painting by Fragonard, became legion. Inspired by these models, crowds of artists transposed him onto plates, bowls, and pitchers; the good-natured face decorated *toiles de Jouy* and snuffboxes; his profile was carved on medals and lockets, and his inelegant silhouette pressed on biscuit, bronze, wax, earthenware, and glass. Franklin's bronze effigy decorated clocks and andirons, making him a kind of divinity of hearth and home, and as the Revolution dawned, he found a place on the murals of a café just off Boulevard Montmartre, cheek by jowl with Rousseau, Voltaire, Helvétius, and Pope, all painted life-size.

So it was that when—on July 11, 1790—Mirabeau announced to the National Assembly: "Franklin is dead," a shiver ran through the audience. Pausing to control his emotions, Mirabeau went on: "He has returned to the wellsprings of Divinity, that Genius who set America free and bathed Europe in torrents of light."

The orator attacked times past "when court etiquette demanded hypocritical mourning as the official sign of a sorrow no one felt." In America, on the contrary, every citizen without exception had been called upon by Congress to observe a national period of mourning for two months.

"Gentlemen, should we not join in this truly religious act and take part in this homage rendered to the Universe, to the rights of man, and to the philosopher who has done more than anyone to spread its message throughout the world?"

Mirabeau proposed that black be worn for three days, a motion that was adopted by unanimous applause. The deputies then invited their president to convey the Assembly's condolences to the Congress of the United States.

Homages to Franklin followed one after the other. The Commune directed Abbé Fauchet to express the regrets of the City of Paris. In the rotunda of the Halle aux Blés, which had been wreathed in black, the abbé pronounced a "Civic Eulogy to Benjamin Franklin," with a picture of the deceased mounted on a pedestal behind him. In a tone imitating Bossuet, the ecclesiastical Freemason exalted fraternity, tolerance, and faith, and the "evangelical perfection" of the departed. In the front row sat Jean Sylvain Bailly, the mayor of Paris, Lafayette, Mirabeau, La Rochefoucauld, Arthur Dillon, and the Abbé Sieyès.

Similar ceremonies were held at the Panthéon, the Club des Jacobins, the Masonic lodge of the Neuf-Soeurs, and by such groups as Les Amis de la Révolution et de l'Humanité, summoned for the occasion to the Café Procope, which was transformed into a necropolis, with cypresses and chandeliers veiled with crepe. The Duc de La Rochefoucauld delivered a eulogy at the Société des Amis de 1789, in which he included personal recollections of Franklin, calling up the period when he had known him in London.

Even though Marat tried to ridicule these demonstrations as mere "humbug," they continued unabated for two months. The printers of Paris piously crowned a bust of Franklin and, rather than dwelling on Franklin's glory, an apprentice addressed his colleagues on his role as a simple workman. "Franklin was born poorer than the poorest among you, yet he had the courage not to be ashamed of his poverty." Because of his tenacity, this great man had managed to educate himself. He had provided an example for everyone to follow: to study to keep enlarging one's knowledge, to share books and leaflets since all printed paper had implicit virtue. Printing had furnished the Americans with a powerful leverage against despotism, and Franklin had ennobled it.

The learned societies prepared their eulogies with greater deliberation. Condorcet wrote four drafts before addressing the Académie des Sciences, and with Pythagoras and Franklin as his models, spoke on human perfectibility. And finally, the Société Royale de Médecine brought the flood of eloquence to an end with a speech by Vicq d'Azyr, which began: "As he climbed the ladder of life, Franklin always went up, never down."

The theater, not to be outdone, presented a new play called *The Printer, or a Celebration of Franklin.*

The obsequies for Franklin coincided with the return to Paris of John Paul Jones. The admiral was on his way back from Russia, where he had been cruelly buffeted by the rudeness of the Empress for whose glory he had fought in the Black Sea. His mind full of ill-digested projects and his energies lacking suitable outlet, Jones crossed Poland, stopped at Amsterdam and London, then directed his steps toward Paris. There, his personality overshadowed that of all the other Americans. Only Gouverneur Morris, always suspicious of Freemasons and their democratic notions, aristocratically disdained the new arrival. For all that Jones had been dubbed a knight by Louis XVI and was a friend of duchesses, Morris treated him cavalierly, to the point of claiming that the noble mariner stuttered.

The celebration of the Federation* was fast approaching, and Paris was in a ferment: everyone, men and women alike, wielded shovels and wheelbarrows at the Champ de Mars, each adding his symbolic stone to build the monument to the Kingdom of France, regenerated by liberty in the American image. Even noble ladies and clergy tucked up their skirts and went to work. The foreigners in Paris, who were equally caught up in the excitement, formed a committee comprising

* Actually, July 14, the date of the fall of the Bastille. In 1790, the first anniversary of that event was turned into a national day of celebration that included parades, a mass, and the swearing of a solemn oath of loyalty to the nation.

Englishmen, Spaniards, Indians, Poles, Swedes, Syrians, Sicilians, Sardinians, inhabitants of Brabant, Avignon, the Grisons, Liège, and mysterious kingdoms of Chaldeans and Arabs. A Prussian baron named Anacharsis de Cloots led the group to the Assembly, describing it as the "Delegation of Humankind." One malicious aristocrat described the heterogeneous mob as made up of Swiss porters, Negro valets, and vagabonds in costumes borrowed from the Opéra. The Prussian baron, who claimed he spoke also for the Americans although his group included none, asked that the committee be invited to the celebration. The Assembly gave the motley crowd a warm welcome and assured them they would have reserved seats at the Champ de Mars for the celebration.

United States citizens were confident that their position as allies assured them good seats, far better in fact than those allocated to the international riffraff. On Saturday, July 10, four days before the great day and three weeks after the other foreigners had been accorded places, the Americans appeared before the orator's desk at the Assembly. The president announced that Admiral John Paul Jones, accompanied by several American citizens, requested admission. The delegates granted his wish, and the noble sailor strode in confidently, with Colonel Swan, Colonel Blackden, Joel Barlow, and William Henry Vernon at his heels. The admiral saluted, then introduced young Vernon, who would speak for them since his French was the most fluent.

Vernon, the son of a rich Newport merchant, had stayed so long in Paris that his father was in despair. He had worn out his epistolary eloquence pleading with his son to return to the United States, promising to pay his debts if only he would come home. But both appeals and promises had fallen on deaf ears.

Vernon chose his words carefully for their impact on his audience: "Struck with admiration for the courage with which you have dedicated yourselves to spreading the principles of liberty, we citizens of the United States are here to testify our deep gratitude and profound respect before the National Assembly." He described the deputies as fathers of a great people and "benefactors of the human race," not forgetting to include the King in his praises. Then he continued:

> We have only one wish left, and that is to be granted the honor of attending the august ceremony that will forever ensure the happiness of France. When Frenchmen shed their blood in the defense of liberty, we came to love them. Now that they are free, we feel in our hearts that we are brothers and citizens together.

The Americans, he said, wished to stand with their brothers before the country's altar where they could "reaffirm their oath of loyalty to the Nation, to its Laws and its King."

The left side of the Assembly broke into applause, soon followed by all the delegates. Then President de Bonnay answered: "In helping you win your liberty, Frenchmen learned to know it and love it. The hands that broke your chains were not made to wear them." His voice filled with emotion, the marquis went on to praise the monarch whose virtues and patriotism had permitted them to win their liberty without shedding "the rivers of blood that were spilled during the American War of Independence. . . . Courage broke your chains; reason, ours."

A thousand voices rang out to approve the motion that United States citizens would occupy the choicest seats at the Champ de Mars. Then, from the heights of his rostrum, the president pronounced the desire that henceforth Americans and Frenchmen be one single people. At these words, the general enthusiasm exploded and Robespierre had to wait for the audience to subside before rising to say, "I should like to make a proposition."

But Robespierre was out of step with his audience. There were murmurs when he described them as "American deputies"; he changed it to "the delegation from the United States," but the murmurs grew louder. The audience tried to prevent him from going on, even though there was nothing in his polite and inoffensive remarks to give cause for alarm. So he let it go with a request that Vernon's speech be printed, since he had spoken the language of liberty with unmatched nobility and passion.

"That is what inspires me to say with understandable boldness—" But Robespierre was too precious and long-winded for this crowd, and their noise drowned him out. The ringing of the bell brought an end to the disorder. The Americans retired, bowing ceremoniously, and Jones and his compatriots were applauded as they left.

The Duchesse d'Anville, meanwhile, invited William Short to spend a few days at La Roche-Guyon. He postponed his visit until after the celebration. Nothing on earth could have made him miss Talleyrand's Mass or the King's oath.

Once at La Roche-Guyon, Short entertained the guests with an account of the ceremony and the evening festivities that had spread to the Champs Elysées, outside the walls of the Hôtel de Langeac. The celebration had everything: garlands of lights strung from tree to tree, lanterns and bonfires, bands and dancers, and athletes shimmying up greased poles to pluck the tricolored flag from the top.

Short used the leisure offered at La Roche-Guyon to

convey his impressions to Gouverneur Morris, then in London for a spell: "The spectacle of that day considered as a spectacle was really sublime & magnificent. The most perfect order & harmony reigned as well then as at the illuminations & balls."

The splendor of the occasion had its seamier side too:

> The streets & Palais-royal presented every evening during the course of the week such collections of people in uniform, returning after numerous dinners & parading with women they picked up in their way, as excited reflections of a disagreeable nature to those who wished to see a patriot & sober legislator in every "fédéré" (you know this is the name of those new deputies). Instead of this, the Palais-royal had the air of the general "rendez-vous" of all the votaries of Mars, Bacchus & Venus.

On the other hand, Short gave credit to the *Fédérés* for their loyalty to the King, but found the passivity of "the Assembly's demagogues" disquieting. He accused them of putting off all decisions concerning future elections: was it possible that they were seeking "to prolong indefinitely" the legislature? Then he added: "It is natural enough to suppose that any body of men whatever who concentrate on themselves all sorts of power, will not be readily disposed to descend from such a height."

According to Short, Lafayette had conquered the *Fédérés* with the simplicity of his manner:

> The Marquis de Lafayette seemed to have taken full possession of the "fédérés." When I left Paris he was adored by them—that moment may be regarded as the zenith of his influence—but he made no use of it, except to prevent ill. The time will come perhaps when he will repent not having seized

64

that opportunity of giving such a complexion to the revolution, as every good citizen ought to desire.

Short ended his letter on a flattering note. Before leaving
for the country, he had paid a visit to the Duchesse
d'Orléans, as always faithfully attended by her lady-in-wait-
ing, Mme. de Chastellux. "You are their 'Magnus Apollo' in
whatever relates to politics & government & revolutions—
they quote you frequently to prove that the constitution can
never march—notwithstanding the new song *'Ça ira, ça ira.'*"

The celebration of the Federation marked the Hôtel de
Langeac's swan song. Jefferson asked Short to dispose of his
staff and the stables, send his furniture and books back to
America, and cancel the lease.

M. Petit supervised the removal of his master's belongings,
and once everything was put to rights, Jefferson invited him
to come to Philadelphia to work for him there. Petit
hesitated; such a voyage, granted it was less risky than going
to the Scioto, made him fearful. Wouldn't he do better to
retire to the country and enjoy his old age in a simple house?
He mulled over his decision as he watched the movers crate
chairs covered in Utrecht velvet, a handsome *méridienne* in
crimson satin, marble-topped tables and commodes, mirrors,
chandeliers, a canvas entitled *The Four Paintings in the Master's
Office*. Lafayette's portrait, which Jefferson had commissioned
from Boze, was already on its way; he had paid the artist
sixteen louis; the crating cost him twelve.

Jefferson also asked Short to buy him wallpaper at the
royal works: a few rolls in "ash-blue," others of climbing
roses on a white trellis. He also ordered draperies of printed
fabric in brick and crimson, some bottles of champagne for
Washington, and for himself, vanilla and olive plants.

Short went to the Comte de Langeac to obtain a cancellation of the lease, but the venal owner demanded such exorbitant terms that the crates were ready for shipment before an agreement could be reached. The comte forbade their removal since the furniture served as collateral on the rent, and authorized Short to sublet the house if he could find a tenant able to furnish it adequately. Their business representatives finally resolved the impasse, and Short was able to turn his attention to sorting out the legation's archives and his own personal effects. He moved with his valet to the Hôtel d'Orléans, a furnished house on the rue des Petits-Augustins. Despite all these preoccupations, he continued to attend to his regular work, followed the debates at the Assembly, visited the Société de 1789, and saw his friends.

The Hôtel d'Orléans had one great advantage: it was near the small Hôtel de La Rochefoucauld. To visit the duchess, he had only to cross the garden—no need to take the rue Jacob and pass through the pretentious entrance of the ducal mansion on the rue de Seine.

While the diplomatic activities of the United States were shifting to the Hôtel d'Orléans, the American merchants in Paris continued their efforts to encourage trade between the two countries. As new laws and regulations were passed, they concentrated particularly on the abolition of the salt tax, which affected the price of salt foods.

James Swan was still involved in trying to provide Frenchmen with their daily bread, but to this he had added new projects. One involved the island of Santo Domingo: he wanted to bring to Paris its raw sugar and rum for refining in a factory in Passy—Franklin's former place of residence.

But Colonel Swan's ambitions went beyond bread and rum. During the year 1790, the United States had begun to repay its debt to France, a result of the arrangements between Short and the Dutch bankers. In order to facilitate payment by a destitute America to a France in desperate need of cash, Swan conceived the idea of setting up a financial group that would take over the American debt. When no cooperation was forthcoming, he temporarily abandoned the project and turned his attention to the French Ministry of the Navy, where he hoped to get a contract for salt foods. He haunted the offices, laid siege to Assembly committees, but in the end he was reduced to helpless indignation at the general corruption. In his journal, Morris wrote: "Swan tells me that he has now the contract in his offer, provided he will admit certain members of the Assembly to a participation. There is, he says, a knot of them who dispose of all things as they list and who turn everything to account. He speaks of their corruption with horror." Swan was not a man who liked to share the proceeds.

Gouverneur Morris dominated the American merchants with his arrogance. He disdained to grovel around French offices like Swan. If he were trying to convert the Navy Ministry to his views on commerce between the Antilles and the United States, he would avoid all contact with the lower echelons and make straight for the minister's office. Like a *grand seigneur,* he considered himself the equal of anyone.

Indifferent to commercial preoccupations, John Paul Jones brooded over his disappointments. Since no navy anywhere in the world would employ him, he pared down his pretensions to the desire for a simple consulate. The United States would soon have need of a consul in Algiers, so he solicited the post. While Philadelphia was considering his credentials, the admiral confided his hopes and sorrows to Short, who encouraged him in the project. Otherwise, he sought out his friends at their homes or in cafés, dined with Lafayette, attended meetings at the Masonic lodge of the Neuf Soeurs, or found comfort with the few ladies who remained faithful to him.

The foolish yet charming young Vernon pursued his carefree ways and flaunted his flowered vests, which caused considerable public comment. One fine day the people's anger exploded, for humble patriots in trousers and wooden shoes judged their enemies by their clothes. Vernon's companion barely saved him from the plebeian fists by swearing on everything holy that the man they had by the collar was not one of the King's henchmen, but an American.

"An American!"

At the magic words, the hands let go and the arms fell. Free once more, the young dandy put his wig and jabot to rights and continued on his way.

A charming young woman soon arrived to swell the ranks of the American colony: Ruth Barlow had finally come to join her husband, but she chose the very moment when his affairs were going from bad to worse. Perhaps her ignorance was due to the slowness of the mails between Europe and America. Inspired by Joel's enthusiasm, she had come over to be on hand for the triumph of the Scioto enterprise, sailing before news of its collapse could reach her. To ready herself for the Old World, which she dreaded, she went first to London, where at least they spoke English. Joel sent Mrs. Blackden to keep her company, with the message: "Tell her I have not slept with anybody but God since I slept with her."

Ruth's delayed arrival suited Barlow well, for it gave his former clients time to vent their rage in other directions—subjects for indignation being plentiful in revolutionary

Paris. Indeed, things improved to such a degree that Joel was able to risk accompanying John Paul Jones to the Assembly. With his affairs a bit less shaky, he went to fetch his wife in England.

Ruth, who had been put off by British manners and by London, was even more disturbed by the charms of Paris. Accustomed to America's vast spaces and the serenity of its cities, and having never lived in anything but sun-filled houses set in gardens, the timorous Ruth retreated into her shell. To her, these cities of the Old World were dens of iniquity, and the stench of Paris revolted her, just as it had Abigail Adams ten years before.

> We are in a narrow, dirty street, surrounded by high houses and can scarcely see the light of the sun. The noise, folly & bustle with which I am surrounded almost distracts me. We have no sabath, it is looked upon as a day of amusement entirely. Tho they work nearly as much on that day as on any other, yet they have mass said every sabath in their churches & many of them are doubtless sincere, and I believe really good folk.

Unable to find such people, Ruth sighed for her own country, blaming Paris for the persistent fever that subsided only when she was asleep. Local custom, which demanded that she be dressed from early morning on and spend the entire day with tiresome people, exasperated her and she longed for the charming informality of the United States. When she took in the fashions, it was only to satisfy her more frivolous friends in New England. "The ladies wear very small caps, hats and bonnets," she wrote her friend Mrs. Timothy Dwight.

She did admire the buildings, the gardens, and curiosities,

but as Joel's loyal disciple, she denounced the sullied source from which the splendors of Paris and Versailles sprang. For Ruth as for Joel, rapacious kings had been able to build their palaces only by mercilessly grinding down the people for centuries, and the example of the court was corrupting to the population. "No person can have an idea of extravagant luxury, folly, wickedness & wretchedness without coming to Europe, this theatre of strange extremes," she wrote to a friend back home.

Her husband's misfortunes did not make Paris any more attractive. In Joel's battle with his creditors, his only exit appeared to be a return to the United States, which Ruth encouraged with all her might. But first he had to untangle his affairs.

In New York, Duer was accusing Joel of every conceivable sin, but he himself was beginning to get engulfed in operations of his own making. At the same time that he was threatening to "unmask Barlow"—who, unlike him, had always been aboveboard—Duer was forced to allow an impartial observer to cross the Atlantic to check the books.

Colonel Benjamin Walker soon declared Joel innocent and Duer guilty, but his examination proved conclusively that the company was ruined. Only William Playfair got out with his skin. Adept at pilfering and juggling the books, Playfair returned to England, where he soon became involved in counterfeiting, hoping that by ruining the value of French money, he could thereby undermine the Revolution.

Unlike his wife, Joel Barlow was all too susceptible to Paris's temptations. He had only to descend four flights of stairs to find himself in the thick of the crowds around the Palais Royal. Under the arcades where Ruth saw only the abominations of Babylon, Joel wandered among the bookstalls, riffled through leaflets, stopped to read the posters, and listened to orators and purveyors of songs. Ever since the journalist Camille Desmoulins, a chestnut leaf in his button-hole, had stirred passersby with his fiery speeches, eloquence had become the fashion everywhere. In vain Joel maintained that he would sail for America as soon as his affairs were in order; the nearer the time came, the less he felt inclined to leave the Old World with all its possibilities and surprises.

# 4

THE BREAK BETWEEN GREAT BRITAIN AND ITS FORMER COL-
onies had brought great hardship to the island of Nantucket,
forty miles off the coast of New England. Before the
Revolution, Nantucket's whalers had supplied a good part of
Europe. As Quakers, Nantucket's people had not partici-
pated in the War of Independence, yet they nonetheless
found themselves the victims of prohibitive new levies
imposed by England on all foreign whale oil. A delegation
sent to London to voice their grievances had run into a stone
wall: England had no intention of lowering the duty by so
much as a penny.

William Rotch and his son Benjamin, the spokesmen for
the whalers, then asked if the hundred families facing ruin
might be accepted in an English port where they could
continue to practice their profession under the British flag.

Lord Hawkesbury, Parliament's leading commercial nego-
tiator, had little sympathy for these "turncoats"; for all their
pacifism, he lumped them together with the other Americans—with the Rebels—and found their request distasteful.
He did, however, wish to be fully informed, and so he
inquired about the cost of transporting these hundred

families. When told "about 20,000 pounds sterling," Hawkesbury vetoed the proposal.

The Rotches then announced they would bring their thirty ships with them, in the mistaken belief this would bring him around. Instead, Lord Hawkesbury answered that it was quite impossible: British carpenters were in need of work, and he was duty bound to protect native shipbuilding. Any vessel flying the British flag had to be built in British shipyards.

Moving from supplication to intimidation, the Rotches began to threaten him: if they were forbidden British ports, they would ask for asylum in France.

Lord Hawkesbury brushed this aside summarily. "Quakers in France!" A ridiculous idea perhaps, but the Rotches pursued it with a vengeance.

Nobody at Versailles would ever have heard of Nantucket had it not been for Lafayette, who was conversant with everything American. Approached by Rotch, he got in touch with Calonne, Vergennes, and Castries and won them over to the idea of importing the Quakers. The Americans were granted concessions in French waters, and Dunkirk was assigned as their new home. The King granted the unheard-of favor of allowing them to practice their faith without hindrance—and this at a time when French Protestants were considered bastards if they were baptized only by their own pastors. The Quakers would be allowed to worship God according to their lights, they could keep their heads covered when all dutiful subjects of the King had to remove their hats, and they were even excused from kneeling in the dirt when religious processions passed by.

All the same, the arrival of 150 Quakers and seventeen ships in 1785, and the nomination of Francis Coffyn as

United States consul in Dunkirk, aroused little interest in Paris or at court. So when, in September 1790, the name "Nantucket" was heard for the first time at the National Assembly, the deputies asked: Nantucketers? Iroquois? What the devil did these American tribes want of them? All that the men of Nantucket wanted was the liquidation of their debts and a subsidy to encourage whale fishing—which, after all, provided the nation with most of its lighting, candles, and soap. The Franco-American refineries in France were producing to everyone's satisfaction, and thanks to whale oil, Paris and France's larger cities twinkled with lights during patriotic festivals.

With Coffyn's encouragement, the Rotches made frequent trips to Paris to plead with the people's representatives; there was always something that needed attention. The father spoke only English, but his son used his new though imperfect French to badger the deputies "night and day," according to one witness. Their persuasiveness finally paid off: the Committee on Commerce agreed to prohibit the importation of all foreign fish oils, which meant that the Quakers of Dunkirk would henceforth dominate the trade. And as soon as this monopoly was granted, the Rotches promised to return to Dunkirk and their harpoons, and forever leave the Assembly in peace. Unfortunately, although this protectionist measure favored the émigré fishermen, it spelled disaster for their brothers and cousins back on Nantucket.

The Marquis de Lafayette had taken the distant whalers under his wing, and to show their gratitude, they sent him each year a giant cheese made from the milk of their cows. Since this ritual made them his liegemen, he was obliged to rephrase the new regulation so that no Nantucketer was left without protection. In its final form, the decree read: "All foreign fish oils coming from any country other than the United States must pay twelve francs a quintal." Abbé Grégoire gave the text his blessing and placed his signature on it.

Even so, the Assembly was not finished with the Nantucketers. Passing from worldly concerns to the idealistic, the Rotches asked permission to appear before the bar with a delegation to request that, in view of the threat of war, they receive confirmation of their exemption from carrying arms.

The whalers made common cause with Jean de Marsillac, a former medical student at Montpellier who, while an officer in the Royal Army, renounced the sword to become a Quaker. Such was his commitment to the sect that he had published a life of Penn.

Marsillac elected himself leader of the delegation and presented the argument to the Assembly. Though his petition was not to the whalers' liking—they were as punctilious in matters of faith as in the choice of proper harpoons—time prevented them from rewriting it and they accepted Marsillac's text. As the Quaker delegation filed into the Assembly's waiting room, petition in hand, Brissot and Clavière exploded at the sight of their unadorned hats: "Fools! Where are your cockades?"

The two Frenchmen were informed that the Lord disapproved of cockades and all other signs of human vanity, be they decorations, crosses, ribbons, or jewels. But how could Divine Law conflict with a law of the Year One of Liberty that made the wearing of the cockade obligatory? The law allowed for no exceptions; by violating it in this flagrant manner, the Quakers were exposing themselves to the fury of the mob.

The Nantucket Quakers stood firm even as the usher announced their turn and the delegation marched into the assembly hall. Mirabeau, who was presiding, invited the Quakers to approach the bar, with Brissot and Clavière at their heels. Then Marsillac began to read "The Respectful Petition of the Christian Society of Friends, Known by the Name of Quakers." The men of Nantucket asked for a confirmation of the privileges previously granted by Louis XVI. Specifically, they asked to be permitted to continue to serve God according to the simplicity of the primitive church. They wished to put their consciences at rest by obtaining assurances that they would be allowed to abstain from all armed conflict and from participating in public celebrations of military victories. In addition, they wanted permission to refrain from decorating and illuminating their homes on patriotic holidays, and they asked for protection from any difficulties that might arise should the inhabitants of Dunkirk take umbrage at their lack of participation. And finally, since they considered all oaths as contrary to Divine Law, they asked that they be allowed to forgo the many oaths demanded by the King and current practices.

Their refusal to fight for France, their aversion to patriotic illuminations (even though this favored the whale oil market), and their distaste for oaths imposed by constitutional law could well have been taken as so many insults aimed at the new society. Yet the naïve stubbornness of these sailors with their rough hands and tanned skin, shifting from foot to foot in their Sunday best, disarmed the Assembly. The French veneration of Franklin no doubt helped their cause. A legend had grown up around Franklin, and ever since, the Quakers—although most Frenchmen knew nothing of their principles and judged them only by their appearance—represented an elite. They were the favorites among a favorite people, the Americans. The originality of the Nantucketers struck a responsive chord among already well-disposed Frenchmen. Had their requests been even more preposterous, the Assembly would have found it hard to turn them down. The French doted on the picturesque—a precursor of the Romanticism already waiting in the wings.

The meeting ended in a salvo of applause. Mirabeau smiled benignly on their demands, and they retired with all their requests satisfied.

The subject of tobacco prompted far longer discussions than whale oil. Finally the Assembly abolished all taxes on the growing of tobacco and organized its administration and sale to France's profit. The French peasant was now free to plant as much tobacco as he liked, to the detriment of Virginia and Maryland importers. The Americans in Paris raised a storm, which finally forced William Short to protest to the ministry the damage this innovation would cause his country.

For the first time, Lafayette changed his tune and refused to support the American position. His liberal principles compelled him to side with the partisans of free cultivation in the face of a retrograde aristocratic minority opposed to all reform.

Gouverneur Morris moved into the fray, scolded the deputies, and claimed he had an understanding with the commerce and diplomatic committees that protected the importers' interests. But when the two committees refused to hear him, he turned to Short, who had been keeping silent, and challenged him to show his mettle. Finally, without a shred of pity for Lafayette's awkward position between the two parties, Morris took on the marquis. But Lafayette was unshakable; he swore that he would never betray the democratic majority, and his firmness forced Morris to resort to a dangerous expedient. Let the decree pass, argued Morris, since the marquis was determined to vote for it. But once that was done, they could get the King to oppose the measure with his veto. That way, Monsieur le Marquis could vote "yes" with his friends, then go higher and kill the measure.

Lafayette was momentarily disconcerted, but he regained control of himself and, relying on sound logic, demonstrated the inconsistency of the United States's obtaining, "at the King's pleasure," a favor that went against the stated desire of the people's representatives. In the end, he rid himself of the importunate American by promising to work out a compromise with Mirabeau.

The intrigue turned into high comedy when the court party—on which Gouverneur Morris depended—abruptly changed tactics. Because Lafayette's name alone infuriated them, and convinced that he was playing a double game that secretly favored the Americans, they decided to trick the trickster. Turning full circle, they voted en masse for the free cultivation of tobacco in France, something they had held up to public scorn only the day before.

Gouverneur Morris was left totally in the dark until his friend, Mme. de Ségur, clarified the situation. Informing him that the court party was motivated solely by hatred for Lafayette, she added that the gentlemen of the nobility were bent on showing their hostility both to the marquis and to his dear United States, taproot of the revolutionary evil.

The New Year parties allowed Morris some relief from his preoccupations. For one thing, they gave him the opportunity to see one of his countrymen, Lewis Littlepage, American chamberlain to the Polish King. Littlepage was on his way back from Spain, where he had carried out a mission for his royal master. Arriving in Paris on Christmas Eve, he found the city in a festive mood. He admired the illuminations and the shops full of New Year gifts "decorated in the best of taste." Delighted with the city, he decided to stay several weeks at the Hôtel de Paris, which provided comfortable lodgings near the Palais Royal. He spent his time with Count Jean Potocki, and together they visited Princess Lubomirska and paid calls at the Hôtel de Lafayette and various embassies and salons. Littlepage picked up again with William Short, whom he had known as Jefferson's secretary and who made no bones now of his desire to be made minister plenipotentiary.

In January, with the candles dimmed, King Stanislas' messenger was struck by the contrast between his last visit in 1787 and the present. If Ruth Barlow complained of the Parisians' frivolity, Littlepage criticized their careless dress: never, before the Revolution, he wrote to a friend, would anyone have dared show himself *en déshabillé* in public. But by 1791, no one was shocked by informal dress. Another unfortunate sign he noted was the city's loss of animation and the few carriages to be seen in the streets.

The Americans brought him up to date on the Paris colony's activities: he soon learned of Admiral Jones's humble situation, Gouverneur Morris' liaison with the Comtesse de Flahaut, young Vernon's escapades, and Joel Barlow's misfortunes with the Scioto Company. He learned, too, that James Swan, the subject of endless stories, had just obtained (thanks to Lafayette) a fabulous contract to furnish supplies to the Navy Ministry. Casting all shame aside, Swan was inviting influential Frenchmen and distinguished Americans to dinner with shady traffickers, including "a Persian from Damascus" and two pirates who pillaged American cargoes and sold their crews into slavery.

Littlepage listened to this idle chatter, but his chief interest lay in politics, for he was on the alert for information that might be useful to his Polish sovereign. Meanwhile he passed along his impressions to Jefferson. He wrote him that Paris "seemed nervous" and that disquieting rumors were making the rounds, rumors of counterrevolutionary plots and of imminent invasion by the Austrian and Prussian armies. Littlepage thought the political parties were exploiting these rumors: "the aristocrats, to keep up the spirit of their despondent party—the democratic chiefs, from the principle that public confidence is never so implicitly bestowed as in time of real or supposed danger." Whatever the reason, Paris was living in a state of extreme anxiety.

Paris was not alone in its uncertainty. In London, one observer was wholly pessimistic. From the moment the Bastille fell, Edmund Burke, member of the British Parliament, had deplored his countrymen's blind enthusiasm for the French Revolution. Looking about him, he noted unhappily that such a respected scholar as Lord Stanhope had accepted the presidency of a revolutionary society. In Parliament, Richard Brinsley Sheridan (the English Molière) was founding a similar society along with the philologist John Horne Tooke, the scholarly Sir James Mackintosh, and John Stone. This society soon boasted ten thousand members in London alone.

Dissident Christians, forever in conflict with the established church and disdained by the governing class, had also rallied to the new ideas. Their ministers extolled the rights of man from their pulpits, and the faithful responded with an ardor worthy of the Jeu de Paume. Chief among them was Dr. Richard Price, who wrote in 1789: "I could almost say, Lord, now lettest thou thy servant depart in peace for mine eyes have seen thy salvation . . . after sharing in the benefits of one revolution I have been spared to be a witness to two other revolutions, both glorious." But their enthusiasm was tinged with Puritanism, for had not Cromwell and their ancestors brought the monarchy to heel when they put Charles I's head on the block?

His Majesty's government soon began to deal harshly with the troublemakers: Lord Edward Fitzgerald was deprived of his officer's commission for having supported a subscription organized by the Friends of Liberty in France. The young lord crossed the Channel to settle in Paris, leaving behind the police and an increasingly stringent justice.

The October Days fed Burke's intemperance to the point where he felt impelled to put his complaints in writing. He continued in this vein for several months, and at the close of 1790, his *Reflections on the Revolution in France* was published. British liberals and dissident sects reacted furiously to this provocation; protestations mingled with refutations. The women were not far behind: Helen Maria Williams, author of *Letters Written in France*, and Mary Wollstonecraft, champion of women's liberties, threw themselves into the fray.

Thomas Paine could not resist an opportunity to give the retrograde aristocrats a thrashing. He in turn pamphleteered with "The Rights of Man." Soon after, he left London for Paris. There, he was introduced to Mme. Roland.

The Roland family had just left the provinces to bask in the Paris sun, and Mme. Roland held open house for her friends, including Brissot, Pétion, Buzot, and Robespierre. In April she wrote to Bancal des Issarts: "Mr. Paine is here. Our friends have been considering a translation of his short work against Burke, but it appears that one of La Rochefoucauld's secretaries has already started it."

Embarrassed by his ignorance of French and his unworldly ways, Paine was a little out of his depth in Paris salons. Still, they provided a place for making useful connections, and it was in one of these gilded rooms that he met a young colonel related to the La Rochefoucaulds and much admired by Lafayette and Condorcet. His name was Achille-François de Lascaris d'Urfé, Marquis du Chastellet. The marquis had fought in the War of Independence, and such was his democratic zeal and egalitarian bravado that he asked to be called simply "Achille Duchastellet."

Even as Colonel Duchastellet, officer in the King's army, was fraternizing with Thomas Paine, enemy of all kings, Louis XVI and Marie Antoinette felt an ever darker shadow engulf the throne. The words said out loud at the Tuileries remained banal enough, but the silences were eloquent.

The royal family was preparing its escape.

Handsome young Count Fersen came to them with a plan. He would disguise himself as a coachman and remove the royal family by means of a carriage he had hidden on the rue de Clichy in the care of his mistress, Eleanora Sullivan. Eleanora was an adventuress better known for her amours than for her success on the stage, to which her parents, a pair of traveling Italian actors, had introduced her early in life. Her adventures had taken her from Italy to Central Europe, to Paris, and eventually to India, from which she had returned with Quintin Craufurd, a rich Scotsman who paid her bills.

In their confusion, the French sovereigns welcomed any help without regard to who provided it. As Count Esterhazy said of the Queen: "You hang on to anything when you are drowning."

Meanwhile, others were involved in the plight of the royal family. Just before leaving for London in April, Gouverneur Morris learned of a letter addressed to the King that had been published in one of the gazettes. As he read it, every sentence provoked him, causing ideas to spin in his head. Beside himself, he sat down at his desk, picked up his goose quill, and composed a refutation.

Adélaïde de Flahaut had for some time been pressing Morris to write the King and offer his advice. She was in complete agreement with the political views of her American lover, just as she was with those of her "official lover," the Bishop d'Autun, and she deplored the fact that so many pearls of wisdom were dropped unnoted in her salon when useful advice was so badly needed. She kept dinning this into Morris' ears—and to anyone else who would listen.

Moved by Adélaïde's chiding and pleased with his composition, Morris decided to share it with Montmorin, the Foreign Minister. He passed it off as an intellectual game, a simple exercise in rhetoric, nothing more. By minimizing his advice, he hoped it would receive a warmer welcome, for in his heart, he thought it was a stroke of political genius.

Montmorin was impressed by its tone: "I have no doubt at all that their Majesties will take the greatest interest in your text." Morris bowed; Montmorin could do anything he liked with the paper as long as he promised secrecy.

From that day on, through the good offices of his ministers, Morris flooded the Crown with advice. He even went so far as to place two informers at the King's disposal. Well versed in political intrigues, Brémond and Jaubert assumed the task of spying on the Club des Jacobins and spreading rumors around the city that were favorable to the government and the court. The ministry could play on public opinion only through intermediaries without court connections. Who could possibly detect the ministers' voices behind the mask of an American merchant? Besides, it would surprise no one to see Gouverneur Morris fluttering about the antechambers. He was mixed up in so many affairs, and his affairs required such constant consultations with the seat of power, nobody would dream of inspecting his wallet to find, wedged between documents on tobacco transactions and real estate ventures, a note destined for the King recommending he harden his position and raise his voice. Montmorin extended a languid hand, complained of weariness, and took the paper. He was thinking of giving up his post to retire to an opium den, preferably in the United States. . . .

William Short suspected Morris of conducting intrigues, but they concerned him little. His relationship with Rosalie de La Rochefoucauld was coming to a head and, in late May, on a visit to La Roche-Guyon, he declared his love. On his return to Paris he received a long letter from Rosalie that was to establish the pattern of their lives for the next half-century. In it she said: "A thousand reasons come to me to prevent my heart from responding to yours and you must not blame me for trying to stifle feelings that would be dangerous for both of us. . . . Thus you must believe that I should never find peace were I to turn aside from the duties which are marked out for me."

Three weeks later, they went on a literary and sentimental pilgrimage to Rousseau's tomb at Ermenonville, where they communed under the weeping willows before their idol's grave. It was on their way back through Chantilly that they learned of the royal family's flight and capture at Varennes.

Shaken out of their dream, they hurried back to Paris and the city's unpredictable convulsions.

That same day, Mme. Roland was entertaining a few friends. Robespierre arrived "shaken with terror" at the thought of the empty throne; no one had any solution except abdication and a regency. As her guests thrashed out the alternatives, someone mentioned the word "republic." If one is to believe Mme. Roland, Robespierre snorted, bit his nails as was his habit, and asked what indeed a "republic" was.

While Robespierre was twitting Mme. Roland, Thomas Paine—who had just published his "Letter to Sieyès"—was weighing far bolder schemes with Achille Duchastellet. The two men minced no words, and the word "republic" did not frighten them in the least for they had come to know it well in America. So they condemned all kings in general and Bourbons in particular. The fact that Louis XVI was insignificant made him no less offensive than his predecessors, and his flight was the last straw.

When the royal family returned from Varennes, Paris welcomed them with a withering silence: not a sound to indicate whether the King should abdicate. The King had left? *"Vive le Roi!"* The King was back? *"Vive le Roi!"* You had only to press the button.

The monarch resumed his vegetable reign where he had left off. Neither the Assembly, the clubs, nor the man on the street thought to force him off the throne. Paine was in a rage. He was wild with enthusiasm for a republic, and Achille Duchastellet drank in every passionate word. Never had the old pamphleteer had such an attentive ear, or a disciple more willing to cast the first stone.

During his hours of solitude and insomnia, Paine conceived an "Address to the French" whose logic was irrefutable: during the King's absence, Paris had spent four days "in perfect tranquility and mutual trust"; while the throne was empty, the people had shown nothing more than "a profound indifference." From which Paine drew the not unreasonable conclusion that the monarch represented a "superfluity" and that it was important for the nation to throw off this burden.

Achille read the text the next day. It so exactly reflected his own thoughts that he insisted it be printed and distributed immediately. He translated it and placed his signature at the bottom of the page, for an "Address to the French" could hardly come from a foreigner, even an American. But before he delivered the paper to the printer, Duchastellet thought it wise to ask Mirabeau's former collaborator, Etienne Dumont, for his advice. Dumont had been exiled from Geneva for extreme intransigence, but what he read filled him with fear and he urged caution: "Have you consulted Lafayette? . . . or Sieyès?"

Achille had consulted only his passion for liberty and his admiration for Thomas Paine. Dumont abandoned the hothead to his fate, and Achille ran off to the printer.

On July 1, 1791, Alexandre de Beauharnais was presiding at the National Assembly when Malouet spoke up: "Under your very eyes, on the doors of the Assembly, in your corridors, the constitution and public order are being scurrilously attacked. A notice proposes that the people abolish royalty. That notice is signed: Achille Duchastellet."

The Assembly listened as the speaker demanded an investigation of the author, printer, and distributor of the notice. The aristocrats and centrists rallied to the proposition, and the debate was on. Though the word "republic" had not figured in the text, Malouet and his friends declared it "an unspeakable scandal." Their indignation, however, did not ignite the majority and the motion was tabled. As the Assembly was preparing to turn to other business, a single voice rose from the right: "You are applauding abominations!"

Meanwhile, the police had found the offending notices and slashed them to pieces.

Despite the fruitlessness of their gesture, the two men responsible for the "Address to the French" refused to admit defeat. Who cared for a constitution already ripe for the garbage can and betrayed by the King before it could see the light of day? Once they passed beyond the monarchical formula, a republic was inevitable. Paine and Duchastellet were no longer content merely to insinuate the word "republic." Together with their friends Brissot, Condorcet, the editor-printer Nicolas de Bonneville, and Dr. Lanthenas, Paine and Duchastellet vowed to make a new world, a world without kings. Paine and Brissot sought to use the press as a weapon against the monarchy. Having finally unveiled the word, they followed it up with a printed newspaper bearing the provocative title *Le Républicain*. Condorcet, Paine, Brissot, and Duchastellet collaborated on the first issue.

But *Le Républicain* attracted little more public support than the earlier notice. Robespierre accused Condorcet of "trying to misrepresent patriots as agitators" in the scurrilous sheet. "When you distribute a journal entitled *Le Républicain*, everybody's ideas become inflamed. The word 'republic' alone divides the patriots among themselves and gives our enemies the pretext they have been looking for to state that there is a party in France plotting against the monarchy and the constitution."

It was still a timid Revolution, unwilling to look beyond a constitutional monarchy. Its partisans were not yet able to push their arguments to their conclusion, and for all the recent convulsions, the outcome they envisaged went no further than a solemn proclamation of the constitution, followed by a "Te Deum" at Notre Dame. Once that was done, the curtain would come down and everybody could go back to work. The elite had no desire to upset the throne.

Not long after the royal retreat from Varennes, Gouverneur Morris returned from a stay of several weeks in London. He found his Paris friends demoralized: Mme. de Flahaut was in a bad humor and Mme. de Ségur was concerned only with finding a safe haven for her fortune. Morris promptly suggested she dispatch it to the United States and buy land. The house of Robert Morris would be pleased to handle the transaction.

Having taken Paris's temperature, Morris conveyed to Philadelphia his observations about the flight to Varennes:

> This step was a very foolish one, public affairs were in such a situation that if he had been quiet he would have soon been Master, because the anarchy which prevails would have shewn the necessity of conferring more authority. The Assembly also was strongly suspected of corrupt practices, was falling fast in the public estimation. His departure changed everything.

Always eager to be in the thick of things, Morris cudgeled his brains for a plan whereby royal authority might be reestablished. By a regency? But who could serve as regent? The King's brothers had all emigrated, leaving behind only a single prince of the blood—the Duc d'Orléans, himself one of the arch troublemakers. Much better to clear away the roadblocks and continue in the same carriage—for all its deficiencies. He debated the subject with Montmorin, with La Marck, endlessly with the lovely Adélaïde, and using her as intermediary, with Talleyrand. Exhilarated by these conversations, he made plans and composed briefs that Mme. de Flahaut edited to make certain his French was faultless. Even so, such was his frenzy that he sent Louis several notes in English, but it mattered little for the King understood English passably well.

While the antimonarchic cell was quietly forming, the Assembly continued with its study of the constitution. Morris repeatedly warned the King to be on the alert: he must be suspicious of everything, read every text with his eyes open, state reservations, demand modifications. Thus, by pointing out the faults and denouncing the consequences, his eventual consent—when given—would have a manly ring.

Montmorin, who served as a mail drop, conveyed to Louis both the draft of a speech written by Morris, which he found to be particularly well phrased, and a brief the King should study before he agreed to the final act. By this time, Morris had become so active that his previously confidential relations with the court had become an open secret. Adélaïde was in on everything, and everything her peg-legged lover said she reported to her clubfooted lover, until—by way of the pillow network—it found its way to Mme. de Staël.

The thought of a speech written by an American for the King of France was too much for Necker's daughter. She must see it at once. Mme. de Staël invited Morris to visit her, but when he did appear, she was entertaining Abbé Louis. By playing devil's advocate and working on the writer's pride of authorship, she succeeded in getting Morris to pull the speech from his pocket and read it to his eager audience: "Gentlemen, it is no longer your King who speaks. Louis sixteenth has become a private individual. You have just offered him the crown and made known the conditions under which he must accept it."

As the tone grew increasingly stern, Mme. de Staël could no longer hold her tongue: she found Morris too severe and his intransigence revolting. Parroting his hostess, Abbé Louis agreed. At this moment, a footman announced Lady Sutherland, wife of the British ambassador, and Mme. de Coigny. Morris had to read the speech all over again, and then eloquence finally gave way to small talk. But it wasn't long before the speech found its way in a dispatch to the British Cabinet, and furnished the lively Marquise de Coigny with a spicy anecdote.

On July 14, 1791, Paris again celebrated the anniversary of the Bastille, and the King allowed himself to be led like a sheep to the Champ de Mars. The day passed calmly enough, but the next few days saw many a demonstration. A republican petition was left on the nation's altar on the Champ de Mars (the republican idea was growing apace), and this unleashed a wave of disorders. The Assembly ordered the mayor of Paris to disperse all crowds, martial law was proclaimed, and Lafayette and his National Guard fired on the mob. Great confusion ensued and patriots divided into warring groups: Lafayette and Bailly took the brunt of the mob's fury, while everywhere, Camille Desmoulins stirred up the mob's hatred.

The British celebrated the Fourteenth of July after their own fashion: Burke's admirers laid siege to Priestley's house. The scientist barely got out in time. In their disappointment at not being able to lay their hands on him, the mob set fire to his house, burning his library and laboratory to ashes. The Académie des Sciences expressed its sympathy for the victim of the auto-da-fé, and the United States offered him asylum.

This sorry action on the part of Burke's disciples was too much for Thomas Paine. Back in London after the fiasco of *Le Républicain*, his pen went into action again. The Barlows were also in England, intending to return to America with the good weather. But Joel kept putting off the moment of departure. It depressed him to think of living in America when the Old World was going through labor pains. To give up now was akin to deserting to the enemy. Like Paine, he was ready to rush to France at the first call for help. So he abandoned himself completely to his revolutionary enthusiasms. His head throbbing with democratic thoughts, he took every occasion to damn Burke and his gang of antirevolutionary zealots. He found his own arguments so persuasive that he, too, put pen to paper and composed a pamphlet entitled "Advice to the Privileged Orders." In it, he dealt harshly with the governing classes, inveighed against the abuses inherent in aristocratic institutions, and warned the world's leaders to be on guard against the anger of humbler folk. He also treated the subject of religion with a freedom bordering on disrespect.

To see his project through, Barlow decided to stay on a few months more, to the beginning of 1792. Ruth was reconciled, all the more so since—thanks to her husband's influence— she had become interested in current events and shared his hatred of Burke. She had been indignant at the morals of kings, courtiers, and clergy, and she now gave Joel her full support in his fight. Besides, she was proud of his reputation in the liberal circles they frequented, where she in turn was

91

making her own friends, notably Mary Wollstonecraft, the apostle of freedom for women.

Once again, the King swore his loyalty to the nation, and the bells tolled the end of the Constituent Assembly. Henceforth, the constitutional monarchy would be dependent on a legislative assembly.

To Lafayette, the Revolution was over. Because he liked to choose his examples from across the Atlantic, he modeled himself after George Washington at the conclusion of the War of Independence: giving up his command of the National Guard, he returned to civilian life.

Bailly had resigned his post as mayor of Paris, and there were those who now wanted to see Lafayette in the Hôtel de Ville, believing he would be the best link between the Paris Commune and the court at the Tuileries. But the Queen, determined to seize any occasion to show her hatred of Lafayette, stepped in, thus unwittingly assuring the triumph of Pétion, a sworn enemy of the Crown.

Lafayette retired to his Mount Vernon in the Auvergne to play Cincinnatus and devote himself to agriculture. But when invasion threatened in December, Louis de Narbonne, the Minister of War, formed three armies and gave their command to Maréchal de Rochambeau, General Nicolas Luckner, and Lafayette.

The Hero of Two Worlds immediately set off for his headquarters in Metz.

# II
# UNDER
# THE
# CONSTITUTIONAL
# MONARCHY:
# 1792

# 5

ALL IN ALL, LIFE IN PARIS HAD NOT CHANGED VERY MUCH. The people went on about their business, complaining the while, and if the poor still lacked for bread, other citizens were eating very well. Well-placed foreigners had little to complain about. In fact, during the course of a small dinner party, Gouverneur Morris treated his guests to Colchester oysters, Rhine trout, and Quercy partridges. In this world gone awry and lulled by its illusions, social life continued unabated and the court maintained the strictest ceremonial. Around New Year's Day, 1792, Rosalie de La Rochefoucauld wrote Short—who was in Holland at the time—that she was spending the holidays as usual, "visiting and receiving visitors."

This was a low period for the young American diplomat. There had not been a word from America about the empty post of minister to France; he was separated from the object of his deepest affection and letters were slow and uncertain. He listened to the rumors circulating around Madrid, Amsterdam, The Hague, and Paris about his government's intentions, but he was no sooner buoyed by one rumor than he was stricken by the next.

Meanwhile, in his cool and confident way, Gouverneur Morris shamelessly stalked Short's tracks, continuing to send unofficial reports to the President of the United States and his ministers. At the start of the New Year, while some went visiting and others celebrated, and with Short sinking ever deeper into gloom, the words "republic" and "republican" had made such subtle inroads into everyday conversation that Morris could write to Washington: "The Republican Party . . . naturally grew up out of the old jacobine Sect." Although Short knew in his heart that Morris was a schemer, he had no idea of the duplicity of which his meddling countryman was capable; nor did he know anything of the mysterious conversations at Montmorin's, where Morris met with Malesherbes, Clermont-Tonnerre, Bertrand de Molleville, and Lally-Tollendal, a recently returned émigré working with the others to restore royal authority.

Every day, Morris' spies brought him a new harvest of information and went away with new instructions. No shift in the political scene escaped the wily American. He knew in minutest detail the daily squabbles that set the King's ministers against each other: Narbonne, for one, was plotting against Bertrand de Molleville and Lessart and at the same time flirting with such enemies of the court as Brissot and his followers.

In February, Morris was called to London on business and on arrival learned a momentous piece of news. After more than two years of reflection, President Washington had decided to end Short's interim in Paris and had chosen none other than Morris himself to become Jefferson's official successor. By way of consolation, Short was named minister plenipotentiary to The Hague.

His stay in London gave Morris an opportunity to

96

examine the situation from a more distant perspective. From now on, Mme. de Flahaut's lover would have to observe greater circumspection and also greater cunning lest he compromise himself in the eyes of the Assembly and the general public. Washington had already given him clear warning. In his letter to Morris advising him of his appointment as minister, he said:

> Whilest your abilities, knowledge in the affairs of this Country, & disposition to serve it were adduced and asserted on the one hand, you were charged on the other hand, with levity, and imprudence of conversation and conduct. It was urged that your habit of expression indicated a hauteur disgusting to those who happen to differ from you in sentiment; and among a people who study civility and politeness more than any other nation, it must be displeasing. . . .

As he observed the British, Morris was able to assess the degree of popular agitation over the Revolution. Paris was at the center of their preoccupations, and they viewed the Revolution as a call to arms. As in France, partisan feelings divided members of Parliament, ministers, businessmen, courtiers, writers, and the men in the street. Even the French émigrés were at each other's throats.

Thomas Paine was foremost among the American zealots in London at that time. He saw Morris for what he was and lost no time in writing Jefferson: "Gouverneur Morris's appointment is a most unfortunate one . . . as I shall mention the same thing to him, when I see him. He is just now arrived in London, this circumstance served to increase the dislike and suspicion."

Part Two of Paine's "Declaration of the Rights of Man"

had just appeared. The ink on his tract was barely dry when Morris came upon a copy and read it from cover to cover with growing indignation. His temper did not improve when he received a visit from Paine. A dispute broke out and Morris declared that thanks to his inflammatory pamphlet, Paine might well find himself hauled into court and condemned. Paine laughed in his face, convinced that the British people would answer his call and rally to his arguments. "Cocksure" was the way Morris described him: Paine was eaten up with vanity and undoubtedly suffering the effects of too much whiskey.

In his journal, Morris wrote of their conversation:

> I tell him that the disordered state of things in France works against all schemes of Reformation, both here and elsewhere. He declares that the riots and outrages in France are nothing at all. It is not worthwhile to contest such declarations, I tell him therefore that as I am sure he does not believe what he says, I shall not dispute it.

This said, they parted company. Later, drawing from this interview what seemed to him the obvious conclusion, Morris wrote that Paine was doing his best to deserve the honors of the pillory.

In Paris the Assembly was dissipating its energies in endless discussions, while at the Club des Jacobins,* wild-eyed orators denounced the "Austrian conspiracy" in which they implicated King, Queen, court, and ministers. There were disturbing rumors circulating concerning Narbonne, the Minister of War. He was supposedly paying off his debts

---

* Originally founded by the more moderate Lafayette, Mirabeau, and Sieyès, the club was, by 1791, led by Robespierre. By 1792, Jacobin was synonymous with the extreme radical element.

with profits from the sale of military supplies and plotting to have Lessart dismissed from the Cabinet so that he could replace him as Foreign Minister. Still clinging to his seesaw, Louis XVI alternately granted favors to friend and foe, thus further unbalancing his already shaky throne. Finally, on March 9, 1792, he dismissed Narbonne and replaced him with the innocuous Chevalier de Grave.

Mme. de Staël let out a loud protest. To her, Narbonne's disgrace was a far more momentous event than the fall of the Bastille, for she attributed to her lovers an Olympian genius equal only to her own. When Narbonne returned to his army post immediately after his dismissal, her heated imagination concocted an epic romance in which her beloved was dressed up as an allegorical Saint Michael, the righter of wrongs. As she saw it, he would forget his grievances, and remembering only his royal origins—illegitimate though they were—and his duty to the Bourbons, would save France by capturing Louis XVI and, placing him at the center of his army, march on Paris to restore the much-maligned constitution.

But even with Narbonne in the army, the situation continued to deteriorate, and there was little Mme. de Staël's friend could do about it. The patched-up Cabinet was on the verge of collapse, and the King was thinking of replacing it altogether. While candidates for ministerial portfolios jostled each other, Terrier de Monciel sent Jaubert, one of Morris' factotums, to London to apprise the American minister of developments and to ask his advice. Jaubert crossed the Channel with a list of prospective ministers for Morris' comments. Monciel's name was high on the list; were the King to offer him a portfolio, should he accept or refuse? "Accept," replied Morris, "but Foreign Affairs only."

Jaubert did not hide the fact that Monciel preferred the

Interior, and added that Foreign Affairs seemed earmarked for Barbé-Marbois. Morris was horrified; Monciel should at all costs avoid getting bogged down in Interior. Moreover, Barbé-Marbois should be ruled out; he was not man enough. They must find a more energetic War Minister, for the Chevalier de Grave was a total loss. Morris did not mince words, and his tone brooked no contradiction.

Having slept on the matter, Morris was less categorical when he saw Jaubert the following day. Barbé-Marbois had come to see Jaubert before he left for London and had protested his devotion to the King. So Morris magnanimously instructed Jaubert to tell Monciel "yes" to Barbé-Marbois for Interior, for want of anyone better.

Meanwhile, back in Paris, Bertrand de Molleville left the Cabinet, Lessart fell victim to Brissot, and the King was forced to form a new Cabinet. But he did not heed Morris' directives, and everybody's schemes fell apart. In point of fact, the Girondists* had secretly put together a Cabinet of their own, with Roland—husband of the famous hostess—at its head. Once again Louis XVI bowed to the will of his enemies and accepted a Cabinet made up of little-known men whose very existence he had barely suspected the day before. Only the presence of General Charles-François Dumouriez at Foreign Affairs offered him some consolation.

Gouverneur Morris took up his functions in Paris at the beginning of May. William Short handed over the reins somewhat ungraciously and briefed him on the current

---

* Backers of a republican form of government as opposed to the existing constitutional monarchy, the Girondists included among their number Brissot, Condorcet, Dumouriez, Vergniaud, and Roland. It was they who prevailed on the King to declare war on April 20, 1792.

business of the legation. On the other hand, Admiral John Paul Jones and Colonel Swan hastened to congratulate him, and his many French friends wined and dined him. The new United States representative resumed his affair with Mme. de Flahaut and circulated about the salons again. Never had his days been so full: he studied the files with Short, haunted the ministries, drafted reports to his government, and as in the past, continued to receive daily visits from his informers Brémond and Jaubert.

Morris' nomination was not greeted with the same enthusiasm everywhere. The gazettes described him as nothing but a backstairs adviser to Louis XVI, and America's warmest friend, Lafayette, indicated little satisfaction—as Morris' obliging friends were quick to tell him. All manner of rumors agitated the little American colony: Saint-Jean de Crève-Coeur reported that Dumouriez refused to recognize the diplomatic status of the new minister, and James Swan replied that this was a groundless rumor spread by Short out of pique.

As for Short, he had not only been outwitted by the perfidious Morris, but he was being forcibly separated from the Hôtel de La Rochefoucauld and the Château de La Roche-Guyon. Yet he remained loyal to his successor, and before departing for The Hague, he introduced Morris to Dumouriez and the three men worked out the details for Morris' presentation of his credentials to the King. In Morris' words:

We go to the Minister of Foreign Affairs. The interview here is very short. I tell him that I have a small favor to ask of the king, which is that he will receive me without a sword because of my wooden leg. He says there will be no difficulty as to that matter and adds that I am already acquainted with the king. I reply that I never saw his Majesty but in public nor ever exchanged a word with him in my life, altho some of their gazettes have made me one of his ministers. Upon this he says that since I have mention'd it he will acknowledge that such is the general idea.

Dumouriez insisted: "The public is convinced that you are in touch with the King." Rising to his full height, Morris protested that he was entirely straightforward in his dealings, and if he had suggested possible improvements to the constitution—unsuccessfully, he might add—he had done so as a private citizen purely out of sympathy for the French nation. But, lest they need further assurance, his new functions would henceforth preclude any intervention in the kingdom's domestic affairs.

And so it was that for the first time in the country's history, a Christian ambassador presented himself swordless to the King of France. Unarmed but proud of mien, the American envoy was received by His Majesty in full regalia surrounded by his courtiers. On receiving Morris' credentials, Louis limited his comments to an awkward "Ah, they are from the United States." He then fell silent while Morris replied, full of assurance: "Yes, Sire, and I have been charged by my government to express the affection of my country for your Majesty and the French nation." As the King made no reply, Morris made the bow required by the rules of etiquette and moved on to the Queen. After a brief exchange of banalities, she presented Morris to her son, and it now fell to the future Louis XVII to carry on the conversation. To round out the ceremony, Morris, the son of a Huguenot, attended mass, then rushed off from the chapel to pay a visit to Mme. de Flahaut, still wearing his court trappings.

The same evening, Rosalie wrote to Short: "You will find this hard to believe, but this morning your successor bestowed on me from a distance the most obliging look in the world, which I answered with a curtsey that was honest but brief. Happily there were too many people between us for him to come over and talk to me, but the mere sight of him caused me great pain."

The next day, Morris dined at Dumouriez's, where he looked with disapproval at the company, the new democratic manners, and the dreadful food. What could one hope for from a Foreign Minister who did not know how to live? The required visits to his colleagues of the diplomatic corps were far more to his taste, for a delicious aroma of the Ancien Régime emanated from the ambassadors' kitchens. Dumouriez's fare was pitiable next to that of the Venetian envoy, for example, with his priceless chef and a wine cellar fit for the gods. Nor did Morris miss a single one of the King's Thursday and Sunday levees, ceremonies that had been transferred from Versailles to the Tuileries without the slightest concession to changing times, though it was obvious their days were strictly numbered.

Determined to live in a style befitting his station, Gouverneur Morris began to search for a suitable residence. His choice fell on an *hôtel* at 23 rue de la Planche near the rue du Bac in the Faubourg Saint-Germain. It had long been the home of an English nobleman, Henry Seymour of the family of the Dukes of Somerset, who was one of Mme. du Barry's last lovers. Before returning to London, Seymour had entrusted his affairs to Perrégaux, the Swiss banker, and as Somerset's agent, Perrégaux went over the lease with Morris and signed it with him.

As soon as Morris was in possession of his palace, he set

about remodeling the interior with the help of an architect. Since he had the personal fortune to back up his pretensions to the highest social strata, he began to make the rounds of the cabinetmakers, upholsterers, chandelier makers, clock makers, and weavers, with Mme. de Flahaut always at his side. As they drove about in his carriage, they made good use of their tête-à-têtes. On one occasion, he wrote: ". . . on the Quai between the Louvre and the Tuileries we again embrace. Had the coachman turned his head, he must have viewed this edifying scene." But Morris' coachman was too well trained to turn around when Monsieur had a lady in his carriage.

One outing took the lovers to the convent at Chaillot, where Adélaïde wished to pay her respects to the nun who had taught her English. While a nun went to find the old sister, who lived at the other end of the convent, her two visitors decided to relieve the tedium of a long wait by making love in the parlor. The fear of being discovered added as much piquancy to their pleasure as the devilish delight of sinning at the foot of the crucifix. Once home, Morris duly noted in his journal this sacrifice to Venus in the House of God.

The American ambassador was eager to start entertaining. While the silversmiths engraved Morris' initials on his flat silver and the seamstress embroidered monograms on his linen, the ambassador addressed himself to the choice of domestic staff and horses. Then, in the evenings, he would relax by taking Adélaïde to enjoy the spring air in the Bois de Boulogne or La Muette, or to dine at Marly. Sometimes they went to the theater where they especially enjoyed a parody of *Lucrèce* that was very fashionable at the time.

The changes in Morris' circumstances caused him a few

inconveniences. For one, Martin, his valet, refused the prestigious title of *maître d'hôtel* because he had not been furnished with a manservant of his own. Infuriated by his insolence, Morris obtained the services of a more modest man to supervise the lackeys and kitchen staff, the coachman and the grooms, not to mention the gardener—for the house was surrounded by flowerbeds. With the problem of the *maître d'hôtel* solved, Morris and his tailor concentrated on the choice of color for his servants' livery and the proper lace for their jabots.

Very different thoughts preoccupied two other Americans during that spring of 1792: Colonel John Skey Eustace, a New Yorker, and Colonel George Schaffner had entered the Revolutionary lists on opposite sides of the barricade, one to defend the Revolution, the other to combat it. And thus it was that these two soldiers emerged from the ranks to appear briefly on the stage of history before oblivion reclaimed them.

At the age of fifteen, Eustace had left school to join the American Revolutionary Army. He fought first under Lafayette's friend General Green, then under Generals Lee and Sullivan, and left the military at the end of the war with the rank of colonel. He first went south to Georgia, then on to the Spanish possessions. But Venezuela so horrified him that he rushed to Madrid to denounce the Spaniards' abominable colonial practices. The Castilian court was, however, indifferent to the abuses he claimed to have suffered at the hands of local petty tyrants. Weary of the battle, Eustace left Madrid after months of futile protestations, and in 1789 he went to Bordeaux.

Eustace was a handsome man, fluent in French and Spanish and given to studding his conversation with Latin quotations. He became more Gascon than the Gascons, yet continued to march in their local parades in the full uniform of an American officer, complete with decorations. But before long his arrogance got him into trouble, for he was sensitive to a fault and took offense at the smallest slight. When some ill-advised business ventures put him in debt, he prevailed on the American consul in Bordeaux, Joseph Fenwick, to help him out of his difficulties. But he took such advantage of Fenwick's kindness that he exhausted the consul's patience. Thereupon Eustace wrote him a blistering letter full of insults and Latin phrases, which he had printed at his own expense and distributed on the Quai des Chartrons. Finally, he carried his outrageous behavior too far: he struck a local dignitary with his cane in a public garden during a military review and was packed off to jail.

Since there seemed to be little future for him on the banks of the Gironde, Eustace decided to return to the United States, where—or so he said—important business had called him. A startling piece of news stopped him in his tracks: the King had declared war against the "King of Bohemia and Hungary," a euphemism employed to spare the feelings of Marie Antoinette's brother, the King of Austria. When this announcement appeared in the local gazettes, Eustace, who was as quick in his decisions as he was with his fists, immediately set off for Paris.

Before leaving Bordeaux, Eustace took the precaution of calling on several well-placed patriots to obtain letters of introduction to influential men in Paris. One of these was addressed to the Minister of Finance. Like Eustace, Clavière was foreign-born and a Protestant, and he proved most accommodating. After describing his military campaigns and service record, Eustace reminded the French minister that France had rushed to America's side to help her defend her liberty and that was why his conscience now dictated that he defend the frontiers of French liberty in times of equal peril.

Charmed by Eustace's enthusiasm, Clavière recommended him to his colleague Joseph Servan, the new Minister of War, who was equally taken with the American. The mere fact of his nationality was enough to soften hearts. The War Minister listened sympathetically while Eustace, always quick to defend his rights, argued that he should be enrolled in the King's army as a colonel, his American rank. His request was based on precedent, for had not Lafayette and the other French officers who had served in the American army been granted, on their return, the equivalent ranks they had acquired overseas?

Servan allowed himself to be convinced. Eustace signed the papers and was commissioned as a colonel. The very next day, he was given orders to join the Northern Army under Luckner. The eager colonel would have left immediately but for another formality—his oath taking—scheduled for two days later. The delay went against his impetuous nature, and the delights of Paris left him cold. Besides, it galled him to see his high-ranking countrymen content to pay lip service to the French cause rather than take up arms. He whiled away the two days with visits to French notables, then prevailed on the deputy from Nantes to have him admitted before the bar of the Assembly.

And so it was that on June 7, 1792, John Skey Eustace appeared before the deputies and the tribune, who were only too eager to welcome a hero of the American war now a volunteer in the French army. All eyes converged on him as he entered, walked up to the bar, bowed, and began to speak in French. The King, he said, had just paid him the honor of allowing him to serve the French nation while retaining his rank as an American colonel. He professed his undying devotion to France and his love for liberty. Then, having said his piece, he walked out to the sound of loud applause.

Once he had taken his solemn oath, swearing loyalty to King and nation and formally offering to lay down his life for France, Colonel Eustace raced toward Douai to report to headquarters at Orchies. During the course of those fifty leagues, his thoughts galloped to the rhythm of his horse's hooves. Already he dreamed of future promotions. He had become a French colonel with ease. Why stop there? Wasn't it logical—in the land of Cartesian logic—that an officer who had been named colonel in the American army in 1781, and whose rank had been recognized by the French, be first in line by reason of seniority for promotion to the next rank, that of *maréchal du camp*? He would have no peace until he saw his dream materialize.

When he reached Valenciennes, Eustace learned from General Valence that Luckner was marching toward Lille, where his troops were to take the offensive. He immediately set off again, overtook the army, and sought out the most congenial member of the general staff, Louis-Alexandre Berthier, a veteran of the American war who loved the United States. Berthier introduced his new comrade-in-arms to Luckner, an old German soldier now serving the French King, and Eustace found Luckner's warlike bearing and Teutonic accent as disarming as Berthier's friendliness.

The American volunteer quickly made friends among Luckner's general staff. In addition to Berthier, he had the good luck to meet Achille Duchastellet, Paine's friend, and Alexandre de Beauharnais, both partisans of the American concept of liberty. Everyone was extraordinarily kind to the newcomer. He was soon assigned to General Dumouriez's staff and busied himself with buying horses and completing his equipment for his assault on enemy territory in quest of glory and fame.

Ever since the War of Independence, Eustace had remained on good terms with a Baltimore family named Cox, one of whom had died while fighting at Eustace's side. This victim to the cause of American liberty had a son, John Cox, who happened to be in London in 1792, and when Eustace learned that young Cox, now twenty years of age, professed a great admiration for France, he decided to have the boy join him at the front. And so, with his family's permission, John Cox left England for Dumouriez's headquarters, where his countryman immediately took him in charge and saw that he was enrolled in the officer corps of the Northern Army.

With his responsibilities well in mind, Eustace kept the Cox family fully informed of their son's doings. He would see that John was properly equipped for the campaign, and as soon as the army was installed in its winter quarters, he would obtain a tutor so that young Cox learned French. Once he had mastered the language, Eustace would see that he received a captain's commission. In the meantime, Dumouriez made Cox a second lieutenant in the 83d Infantry Regiment, and on October 23, Eustace took him on as aide-de-camp. He wrote Baltimore: "My friend, general Dumouriez, allowed me to take him in addition." He also informed the family that henceforth all mail to the new French officer should be addressed to "Monsieur Cox, American, second lieutenant in the advance guard, in care of General Dumouriez's army." These letters were best sent via London or Le Havre, or if the family preferred, they could use the American ministers in London, Paris, or The Hague as their mail drop.

109

Eustace took care to add that the family need have no fear about John's patriotism. Eustace himself had remained a loyal American, and he would see to it that his protégé's love for his native land remained intact. There would be no question of his following the bad example of those Americans abroad who were so taken with the pleasures of the Old World that they tended to forget their own country. According to Eustace, the young second lieutenant was protected from temptation by his passion for France's liberty, the sound educational principles instilled in him since boyhood, and his great respect for the government of the United States. In the end, everybody was gratified that the young American had been recruited into the revolutionary army.

By a quirk of fate, Dumouriez had three American citizens under his command at the same time: Eustace, Cox, and one Eleazar Oswald, a colonel in the American artillery who had been sent to him by the War Minister in September 1792—"to assist the adjutants-general." The following month, Eustace wrote to the Coxes in Baltimore: "Col. Oswald is here and will be employed, I fancy, in artillery; the unfortunate does not speak a word of French."

An Englishman by birth, Eleazar Oswald had emigrated to America and taken part in the struggle against his own country. He distinguished himself at the battles of Quebec and Fort Ticonderoga. After the war, he turned to journalism and was for fifteen years the editor of an influential Philadelphia newspaper, the *Independent Gazetteer*. It was especially popular in the countryside, for Oswald, like Jefferson, was a staunch advocate of a rural, agricultural America and defended the farmers against the businessmen and bankers so dear to Alexander Hamilton. Oswald did not mince words, nor did he shrink from duels to back them up.

On a trip to Paris, he found his enthusiasm for France and liberty rekindled. Once his countrymen introduced him to the War Minister, he lost no time enlisting in the armies of the republic.

Armand de La Roüerie had been petulantly ignoring the proceedings of the States-General; now he was heaping scorn on the National Assembly and its projects for a constitution. His imprisonment in the Bastille notwithstanding, he had repudiated the cult of liberty and decided to consecrate his life to the restoration of the Ancien Régime. But while others were plotting the destruction of the revolutionary hydra from abroad, La Roüerie was too firmly rooted in the soil of his native Brittany to cross the border. It was his conviction that the nation must purge itself from within, and to that end, he set out to organize the antirevolutionary forces in France.

Schaffner, ever in La Roüerie's shadow, shared his ardor and aspirations, and this bound them together as never before. Once they had laid the groundwork and put the finishing touches on their plans in Brittany, the two embarked on extensive travels, for they needed the assent of the émigrés and the princes if they were to integrate the forces within the country with those outside. They went first to the Isle of Jersey, then to England (where ex-Colonel Armand assumed the name of James Ireland), then on to Holland, and finally to Coblenz, where former Finance Minister Charles Calonne was instructed by the émigré princes to examine La Roüerie's proposals. He quickly saw their merit: a Breton army in France would furnish a welcome complement to the invading forces and facilitate the problem of disembarking troops. When Calonne had communicated his thoughts to the King's youngest brother, the Comte d'Artois, the latter granted La Roüerie the power to recruit a secret army. Having transmitted this news, Calonne advised La Roüerie that discretion dictated he leave Germany as soon as possible. Once in Paris, La Roüerie was to await a messenger who would arrive with detailed instructions and the funds necessary for the venture.

When Calonne's messenger met La Roüerie in Paris, he informed him that a supply of arms was on its way to Brittany by sea and gave him a large sum in foreign currency, which he was to convert into French money as inconspicuously as possible. Too much of a gentleman to dirty his hands with money matters, La Roüerie sought out an intermediary to perform the transaction. His thoughts turned back to Dr. Chevetel, who for the past two years had been official doctor to Monsieur, the King's brother, and a wily fox if there ever was one.

Monsieur had just emigrated, but his farsighted doctor had already left his service to set up a practice near the old monastery of the Cordeliers where he lived contentedly with Mlle. Fleury, replacing La Roüerie (and several others) in the actress's affections. This in no way prevented La Roüerie from taking up with Chevetel again, and as the marquis never supposed for a moment that a former vassal might hesitate between the true cause and that of the mob, he confided to the doctor his plans for a clandestine Breton army that would aid and abet the coalition marching on Paris to restore Louis XVI to his legitimate rights. Having told him his military plans, La Roüerie asked the doctor if he happened to have any connections with money changers and the like.

Taking great care not to give himself away, Chevetel readily agreed to help in any way possible. But the mission was not to his liking, for he had little appetite for a losing

112

cause when a winning one was at hand. Now that he was living in the shadow of the radical Club des Cordeliers, he had come to admire his neighbor Danton and was proud to shake his hand when they met in the street. He remembered only too well how it felt to sit at the far end of the table when, as a timid country doctor, he was granted the honor of dining with his lordship. Yet, after all these years, he still was a liveried valet at heart and clicked his heels the moment La Roüerie raised his voice. So he changed the money and waited for the propitious moment to tell Danton what was afoot.

La Roüerie and Schaffner set off for Brittany weighted down with *louis, écus,* and *assignats.* As soon as they were back at the château, La Roüerie named Schaffner adjutant-general and sent the nomination to Calonne for the princes' ratification. From then on, a constant flow of emissaries moved between the Château de La Roüerie and Coblenz and between Jersey and London.

The Comte d'Artois formally approved the marquis's battle plan, but his ratification of Schaffner's commission was longer in coming. The dossier hung in suspense for several months, and it was not until May 1792 that Calonne dispatched the following letter:

Monsieur de Schaffner:

Having been informed of the reasons, based on your meritorious service, as well as on your experience and military valor, that have led the Marquis de La Roüerie, in accordance with the powers vested in him, to name you adjutant-general of the Breton Association, we approve and ratify said nomination and desire and command that you be so recognized and obeyed in this capacity. In witness whereof, we have signed the present confirmation and set the seal of our arms thereto.

113

And so, if the Marquis de La Roüerie and "Monsieur de Schaffner" still continued to "forage" through the woods, they were now after bigger game. Their efforts were crowned with success when the volunteers gathered at the Château de La Roüerie at Whitsuntide in 1792. The marquis counted his recruits and held open house to the sound of clattering plates. Wine flowed freely, German and English coins clinked in the guests' pockets, while outside, their horses whinnied in the stables. Later there were midnight excursions in disguise, *noms de guerre,* passwords, and rallying calls. Some Amazons in plumed hats lent a theatrical air to the conspiracy—to the delight of the crowd in the great hall. Tree trunks and piles of brush blocked the approaches to the château; lookouts manned the entrances to the property, and from time to time, an owl hooted in the shadows.

The night of May 28 the crowd exceeded all expectations. Such a parade of people marching across the countryside could not fail to attract attention. The local authorities were alerted and a police raid organized. But when the constabulary arrived at the château, they found no one. Forewarned by his spies, the marquis had cleared out his troops, and he and Schaffner had gone into hiding with a neighbor.

The government of the *Département* gave up the search, and life went back to normal. But two months later, the same authorities ordered house raids on various suspects. Once again, La Roüerie escaped; however, a lieutenant and sergeant from a company of gunners at Vitré found "two individuals in bed" and demanded to see their papers. One of the strangers produced two passports, both in the name of George Schaffner, but each one assigning him a different nationality. The investigators duly noted: "Confusion concerning the identity of M. Schaffner, either French or

114

American, led us to decide that he should be taken into town." The suspect's bedfellow, "Sire Tuffin," one of La Roüerie's cousins, was brought along as well.

When his jailer brought him before the magistrate at Vitré, the man with the two passports affirmed that he was indeed George Schaffner, thirty-three years of age, that he lived off his assets, and was a resident of the Château de La Roüerie. The clerk of the court noted: "When asked if he was French and had always lived in France, suspect replied that he was born in the city of Lanquaster in the province of Pince-la-Vannie, on the continent of La Merique."

And why was he in France? Schaffner answered that he had fought under La Roüerie in America, that they "had become fast friends and had resolved to spend the rest of their days together." They had not parted company in eight years. And why did he have two passports? Well, the municipality of Dol, which had jurisdiction over Saint-Ouen-La-Roüerie, had issued the first passport; but, being little educated in such matters and ignorant of the law, the municipal authorities had attributed him French nationality. When he realized the error, Schaffner felt obliged to have a second passport issued in the district of Fougères, reestablishing his true nationality, which was, in fact, American.

The judge then asked the dread question: "When did you leave La Roüerie, and why?" Schaffner had learned his lesson well. It had been rumored in the region, he replied, that the National Guard was marching on the château to burn it to the ground. "We were afraid, and so we left." The questioning then went farther back in time: had Schaffner spent the preceding winter at the château? Had he not been traveling about in La Roüerie's company?

With the same look of innocence, Schaffner replied in his

115

best French that his host had taken him to visit various members of his family, and also to oversee his landholdings. During the course of the previous year they had been away together for a longer period—they had gone to Holland, via Jersey, and had later stayed in Paris. As for the large gathering at the château over Whitsuntide, that was a figment of people's imaginations because, in reality, there had been no one there but a few friends and relatives come to take refuge from the brigands abroad in the countryside.

Schaffner then fell silent, the judge's tone hardened, and the clerk noted down with his scratchy pen: "Pointed out to the defendant that it was useless to hide the truth." In fact, the magistrate had no illusions concerning the concentration of armed men at the château and was only trying to get a few names and identify the conspiracy's ringleaders. Schaffner, however, continued to protest that he had noticed nothing the least bit unusual at the château. What is more, he had been taken ill and confined to his bed during Whitsuntide, with no one but his host and the servants allowed access to his room.

The whole affair was proving to be too much for the municipal authorities in Vitré. Had they or had they not laid their hands on a dangerous conspirator? Unable to determine the importance of their catch, they transferred the mysterious stranger to the jail at Rennes, the nearest city, and with all the respect due his station, provided him with a military horse and an escort of two gendarmes. On his arrival at the courthouse, he was charged with aiding and abetting the unlawful enlistment and assembly of armed men and was brought before the local tribunal. Here the magistrate recorded his civil status and physical description a second time: "Height, five feet five inches, brown hair and eyebrows, blue eyes, normal nose (a bit thick), average mouth, cleft chin, high forehead, round face." And then the grilling began again.

Had he not been aware of the cannons, rifles, and ammunition stored at the château? Had he not seen the lookouts standing guard day and night at the barricades built across the avenues leading into the property? Did he know nothing about the enlistment of peasants and the distribution of money? Schaffner stood his ground; he had seen no arms other than hunting rifles and no ammunition except for a few pounds of gunpowder, also used for hunting. He had indeed observed a few piles of brush between the stables and the barnyard, but why should a minor detail like that have bothered him? As for the alleged enlistments and distribution of money, no news of these had reached his ears. Nor, finally, did he have the slightest idea where La Roüerie was at that moment.

The judge gave Schaffner a severe tongue-lashing, turned to the clerk, and instructed him to record: "Pointed out to the defendant that he is not telling the truth, that he has private knowledge concerning these gatherings but does not wish to reveal their purpose." How could an American stoop so low?

Schaffner protested his sincerity. At this point the tribunal intensified the debate and asked Schaffner his opinions of the French Revolution, of equality and fraternity. Schaffner replied by recalling his American campaigns and his fight for the independence of his own country, for the triumph of liberty and equality. And, he added, he would always remain faithful to the ideal of universal freedom.

The magistrates nodded their heads while he signed his statement. Of course there was no doubt that the rogue was lying when he denied any knowledge of the gatherings at the Château de La Roüerie, but it was equally obvious from the passion in his voice that his love of liberty was genuine. In the end, the old French weakness for the United States weighed in Schaffner's favor. This prejudice was so firmly rooted in the minds of Frenchmen, even in the remotest provinces, that the magistrates were moved, against all the dictates of reason, to hand down the following verdict: "In view of the fact that there exists at present no formal charge against M. Schaffner with respect to the unlawful assembly of troops by the Marquis de La Roüerie, we have released him on good behavior."

With that behind him, Schaffner was off to rejoin La Roüerie in his efforts to mobilize the Bretons. As far as Cousin Tuffin was concerned, although he gave less cause for worry than Schaffner and answered all questions in a manner no less equivocal, he was unfortunately a mere Frenchman. The law came down heavily on him, and after a long incarceration, he died on the scaffold.

# 6

At the beginning of June 1792, the king dismissed the members of his Cabinet who belonged to the "Bordeaux Faction," as Gouverneur Morris called Roland's Girondists, and Roland himself turned over his portfolio as Minister of the Interior to Terrier de Monciel. At this, the mob took to the streets again. As Morris wrote to Jefferson, Paris was sitting on "a vast volcano," and he blamed the King's court for being diametrically opposed to anything that suggested liberty, and for doing their utmost to ruin the constitution.

In mid-June, the American minister, accompanied by the British ambassador, Lord Gower, made his last visit to the Tuileries to pay court to Louis XVI. After the King's levee, the diplomatic corps took their places at the Queen's gaming tables. The courtiers circulated from table to table, chatting among themselves, oblivious to the ominous rumblings beyond the palace gates. Morris was disgusted by the vapid ceremonial routine; what was there to hope for from people whom events had left so far behind? He gave vent to his frustration in a letter to Rufus King, the distinguished American politician-statesman who was at that time one of New York's first two Senators. Morris wrote: "The court [is] involved in a spirit of little paltry intrigue, unworthy of anything above the rank of footmen and chambermaids."

On June 20 the royal family was forced once again to drink the bitter dregs of humiliation.* In a letter to William Short, then in The Hague, Rosalie de La Rochefoucauld gave a moving description of the scene:

> At three o'clock, that enormous crowd of people began to act as though at a carousal, uttering frightful cries and demanding to see the King in order to hand him a petition. . . . [The door] was opened in the name of the law and that horde of barbarians hurled themselves into the Château with all their pikes and their scythes. They broke in the doors, brought up a cannon, battered down partitions when the doors were too narrow, and a great number of them entered the *oeuil-de-boeuf* where the King was seated with Mme. Elizabeth, his Ministers, and at most ten or twelve people.
>
> Charles [Rosalie's younger brother], who was one of the number, described this scene to me and said that at this moment they threw themselves in front of the King, sword in hand, to defend him. But when this huge mob rushed into the room, they knew at once that their number was too small to undertake anything and they returned their swords to the scabbards.
>
> In a calm and courageous manner, the King approached them and asked them what they wished. They talked of the veto, that they wished he would give his assent, and they made the most horrible, the most insolent and frightful threats. Without showing the least excitement the King replied to them with all the gentleness and firmness possible,

---

* The war, begun with such enthusiasm, was going poorly. An attempted invasion of the Austrian Netherlands by the French had failed, and by June, the enemy had opened a line of march to Paris. These reverses caused people to suspect the royal family was aiding the enemy. By June 20, tensions in Paris had reached the boiling point.

that this was neither the time nor the place to demand or receive such a proposition. . . . Finally one of these men had the audacity to wish to place the red cap upon his head. The King, however, constrained by the clamors which resounded about him, himself took the red cap from the hands of the man who offered it and put it on just as a bottle was brought him and he was obliged to drink to the health of the nation.

When the last of the mob had been cleared from the Tuileries, Terrier de Monciel turned to Gouverneur Morris for advice. He was preparing an address to the National Assembly in an effort to heal the wounds, and he needed some solid arguments to bring the deputies to their senses and restore order in the streets. Morris promised the Minister of the Interior his wholehearted cooperation; Morris would think the matter over and write him a note.

That day, Morris dined with the Comte de Montmorin, Malouet, and Bertrand de Molleville, and the four men held a council around the table. Morris then returned to the solitude of his office and outlined a speech for Monciel in which he exhorted the deputies to protect the last vestiges of the monarchy before the flames devoured it.

At this juncture, Lafayette left his army post to attempt to salvage the situation. The applause that had greeted Colonel Eustace's appearance before the Assembly a few weeks earlier was a faint rustling compared to the feverish acclaim that greeted the marquis. He completely overshadowed Terrier de Monciel, and optimists thought for a moment that the Hero of Two Worlds had saved the day once again. But the monarchy was too stricken; any attempt to save its life was a waste of time. And the moment was fast approaching when Lafayette himself would throw in his hand and go into exile to extricate himself from a hopeless situation.

The same thought was beginning to occur to certain ladies in Paris: heretofore opposed to the idea of emigrating, they prepared to leave for England. Even the Duchesse d'Anville, William Short learned from his Rosalie, was thinking of moving closer to Rouen because it was guarded by troops under her nephew, de Liancourt, and was also on the way to the coast. Adélaïde de Flahaut, completely demoralized, told Gouverneur Morris that she was ready to follow him to the United States—where he had no desire to take her and no thought of going so soon. Wild horses could not have dragged him from Paris during this crucial moment in history when he still nourished the hope that Louis XVI would rouse himself from his torpor and make a last desperate effort to save his throne. If the King could only be convinced to go to Rouen, where everyone was waiting for him! But no, the royal family vacillated, hearing out all the escape plans and choosing none. If a plan seemed acceptable at first glance, they immediately agreed to it, whereupon new advisers would arrive on the scene and reduce them to uncertainty once again. In the end, the royal family stayed put.

Social life was on the wane. From Raincy, where she was sequestered with her father, the Duchesse d'Orléans wrote wistfully to Morris: "Ah, when will we ever meet over a cup of tea again?"

Tea indeed! But such were the questions that preoccupied people of fashion. The American minister rarely dined out now that so few people were entertaining. Likewise, there were few aristocrats left whom he could impress with his new china, his monogrammed linen and silver, his footmen with their lace jabots, and all his other fine acquisitions.

And over at the Louvre, Adélaïde de Flahaut was packing her trunks. Her American lover having failed her, the lady

122

had fallen back on the Bishop d'Autun and decided to make for England with her son's father, an eminently suitable solution in her eyes. To her husband she gave not a thought.

During the latter half of July, as the regime moved inexorably toward its fall, Paris heard the news of Admiral John Paul Jones's death. The illustrious sailor, who had been ailing, had sent a messenger to Gouverneur Morris to tell him that he wished to dictate his last will and testament in the presence of his country's representative. Morris had dutifully made his way to the rue de Tournon. There Morris found the invalid in a sorry state, his breathing difficult and uneven, his face bloated and yellow with jaundice. Gone was the brilliant John Paul Jones before whom the doors of Versailles had swung open, and who had somewhat pompously proclaimed at the time of his knighting by Louis XVI that he did not wage war to amass wealth, nor as a simple American, but to defend the rights of man and as a citizen of the world. Gone too was the dashing gallant who addressed verses "To the beautiful ladies who have done me the honor of lending me their attention."

Now Jones had only two friends to pay him any attention: Colonel Blackden and a Frenchman, Captain Jean-Benoît Beaupoil de Saint-Aulaire, a Freemason and the author of several pamphlets on liberty. Beaupoil, who had left the King's army to command a "free company" during the American war, loved the United States and took great pleasure in speaking English.

With the formalities of his will taken care of, Jones began to waste away before his witnesses' eyes. Ready to move heaven and earth to keep their friend alive, Beaupoil and Blackden asked Gouverneur Morris to use his influence on

Dr. Félix Vicq d'Azyr, the Queen's physician, and bring him to Jones's bedside. The minister agreed to fetch the doctor, but not before he kept a dinner engagement with the British ambassador. After dinner he made his way to the Louvre, where Mme. de Flahaut was awaiting him, and together they went for the doctor. With all these delays, by the time they arrived at the rue de Tournon, it was too late: John Paul Jones, barely forty-five years of age, was dead.

Vicq d'Azyr certified his death, and Morris and the landlord saw to it that the apartment was sealed. For Jones's friends, however, their difficulties were not yet over. To their dismay they discovered that, revolution or no revolution, no Protestant, not even a hero of two worlds, could be buried within the walls of a Catholic city. Somewhere outside the city, a cemetery for "foreign Protestants" had been established after Louis XIV's death, but who the devil knew where it was?

Finally, after vainly trying the police and the commissioner of the district, Pierre-François Simonneau, the King's commissioner, recalled that the final resting place for heretics had been moved from the nearby Porte Saint-Antoine to the distant fields behind the Hôpital Saint-Louis. In accordance with the laws of a previous era, but a law that nonetheless must be respected, the burial had to be there and only there. The King's commissioner then inquired into the honors to be paid the deceased. His friends explained that since Jones had no immediate family in France, the United States minister was the only person qualified to make the funeral arrangements, and he had just given formal orders that Jones be buried in the simplest manner possible to keep the cost at a minimum.

Simonneau leapt to his feet. A simple little burial for such a great patriot and defender of liberty? The thought was too much to bear, and he declared that he would pay out of his own pocket for a ceremony worthy of the hero. Touched by his reaction, Jones's friends, together with Simonneau, set about to devise a plan. Blackden was delegated to write the president of the National Assembly announcing the admiral's death. His letter concluded with the words: "The admiral's friends await the orders of the Assembly concerning the nature of the burial." The deputies immediately took the matter up, not failing to notice that the minister of the United States had ordered the meanest possible funeral.

The silence that greeted this was heavy with reproach. Simonneau's attitude, however, was applauded. The deputies gave their unqualified support to the contention that a man "who had rendered important service to the United States and France" could not be laid to rest without crepe, flags at half-mast, a funeral march, and a show of arms. A decree followed, describing the funeral procession and designating who was to be in it and in what order. It was decided that twelve members of the Assembly would lead the procession, escorted by an honor guard of grenadiers from the *gendarmerie*. A funeral oration delivered over the grave would bring the ceremony to a close.

The next day the procession formed in the rue de Tournon and, preceded by drums veiled with crepe, made its way down the rue de Seine to the Pont Neuf. The twelve deputies rode in carriages behind the hearse between double rows of grenadiers under a commanding officer. Gouverneur Morris had not seen fit to bestir himself over his illustrious countryman's funeral and had sent Major James Cole Mountflorence, an attaché at the legation, to pay the necessary homage. At the Protestant cemetery on the outskirts of the city, the coffin was lowered into the ground. Pastor Paul Marron, a Huguenot who had recently returned from Holland to which he had been exiled for his religious beliefs, stepped out from the crowd to deliver the funeral oration.

"Legislators! Citizens! Soldiers! Friends! Brothers! and Frenchmen! We have returned to earth the last remains of an illustrious foreigner, one of the first champions of American liberty, that liberty that so gloriously preceded our own." After a few barbs at Empress Catherine of Russia, the pastor celebrated "the sweet pleasures of private life in France" that had charmed Jones, as opposed to "the pestilential air of despotism" that the "Semiramis of the North" had forced him to breathe but which he had not been able to tolerate for long. Marron then turned to the subject of military virtue and glory, remarking that "the fame of the brave man lives after him and his prestige is his immortality." The patriotic pastor continued in the heroic mode, asking in ringing tones: "What more flattering tribute can we pay to the remains of John Paul Jones than to swear over his tomb that we will live and die free men?" In closing, the eloquent voice rang out: "The country is in danger!"

Gouverneur Morris expressed his own view of the proceedings in a letter to Robert Morris informing him of Jones's death: "Some people here who like rare shows wish'd him to have a pompous funeral and I was applied to on the subject, but as I had no right to spend on such follies either the money of his heirs or that of the United States, I desired that he might be buried in a private and economical manner."

That autumn, the flotsam and jetsam the admiral had left behind was sold at auction to satisfy his creditors. His heirs, who lived in England, had asked Morris to look after their interests, and the minister duly sent along a copy of the will

Rosalie, Duchess de La Rochefoucauld.
*(Courtesy of Mrs. J. Everett Eaves, Jr.)*

William Short, by Le Met. *(College of
William and Mary, Virginia. Photo courtesy of
Mrs. J. Everett Eaves, Jr.)*

*The Surrender of Lord Cornwallis* (detail of French officers),
by Trumbull. *(Yale University Art Gallery)*

Joel Barlow, by Vanderlyn, 1796.
*(Musée de Blérancourt)*

Ruth Barlow, by de Villette, ca. 1800.
*(The Connecticut Historical Society)*

Thomas Jefferson, by Trumbull, 1787. *(The Metropolitan Museum of Art, bequest of Cornelia Cruger, 1923)*

Marquis de Lafayette. *(The Metropolitan Museum of Art, gift of William H. Huntington, 1883)*

Thomas Paine, engraved by Sharp after a portrait by Romney, 1793. *(Bibliothèque Nationale. Photo Harlingue-Viollet)*

John Paul Jones, 1789. *(Musée de Versailles. Photo USIS)*

Gouverneur Morris, by Du Simetière, 1783. *(Bibliothèque Nationale)*

Adelaide, Countess de Flahaut, by Labille-Guiard. *(Bibliothèque Nationale)*

on October 22. The seals, he informed them, had been removed by court order at the demand of Jones's creditors, and the sale had ensued in the usual way. Morris had been there in person and had acquired the sword worn by the admiral during his famous victory over the British frigate *Serapis*. He had also bought Jones's military decorations, his Order of Merit, and the Cross of Cincinnatus, and he stood ready to restore the lot to Jones's family on payment of his expenses. As for the sword that Louis XVI presented to Jones when he was knighted, it had been withdrawn from sale and put aside for his heirs.

Baron Grimm, who continued to keep Catherine II up to date on Paris happenings, could hardly omit a description of the admiral who had been in her service. The Empress replied: "John Paul Jones was a rotter who deserved to be honored by a gang of rotters."

That was the end of John Paul Jones, for whom not a single Paris bell tolled. Twenty days later the question of Protestant burials in Paris cemeteries was solved once and for all when the Swiss Guards slain while defending the Tuileries were buried en masse in the cemetery of Madeleine-de-la-Ville-l'Evêque. It prompted no reaction. From that day on, the police regulations were a dead letter.

During July and early August of 1792, Louis XVI gradually yielded to his tragic fate, and the last-minute regeneration Morris looked for never materialized. The King did take certain measures to protect his fortune, and Gouverneur Morris, well shielded by the Stars and Stripes, seemed to him the ideal repository for his gold. Terrier de Monciel agreed, and by the end of July the King's devoted minister was shuttling back and forth between the Tuileries and Morris' *hôtel*, carrying sacks of coin and packets of paper money to safety. On one trip alone, he had half a million francs in his carriage.

Upon delivery, Gouverneur Morris set about converting the *assignats* into gold *louis*, and soon the American legation looked like a money changer's office, with piles of gold everywhere. Morris himself presided over the preparation of five thousand purses to pay for services rendered, and to warm those who were cool to the monarchy. Unfortunately, the regime collapsed before Morris had time to distribute the manna.

The American minister had invited a few people in to dine on August 10. The date was ill-chosen, for by dinnertime, all Paris knew that the Swiss Guards at the Tuileries had been murdered and that the royal family had sought refuge with the Legislative Assembly.* Several guests, reluctant to dine to the sound of cannon fire, sent hasty regrets, while others not invited turned up at the door. A constant stream of desperate people began flooding the legation seeking refuge.

To add to Morris' difficulties, the hot weather had spoiled his fish, forcing him to eliminate from the evening's menu the platter of perch bought that very morning. Nevertheless, guests of quality continued to arrive, and the crush was all the greater because none of Morris' visitors had seen fit to leave home without at least one servant. So while their masters occupied the salons, Morris' livery took care of the visiting valets and chambermaids.

* The insurrection, which began on August 9, was led by the extreme radical Jacobins. They toppled the legally elected commune and established a revolutionary commune in its place, with Danton as its leading figure. On August 10, the handful of deputies left in the Assembly voted to suspend the King from office. The King and his family were imprisoned in the Temple, and anarchy reigned.

Adélaïde de Flahaut sent her son Charles on ahead in the care of a lackey; she herself arrived shortly afterward. That night, they were to meet Talleyrand and leave for London. As usual, she had thought of everything and had made certain her exile would not lack the amenities: the youngest of her three lovers, Lord Wycombe, would take over as soon as she set foot on English soil. Every love affair has its price, and the daughter of Mme. Filleul and *Fermier-Général* Bouret always collected her debts.

The French were not alone in their anxiety. In the American colony, several merchants, including James Swan and Benjamin Jarvis, asked for passports so as to be ready to leave the country at a moment's notice. In her husband's absence, Mrs. Blackden, probably loath to walk the streets alone, sent a messenger to the legation for the same purpose. Thomas Waters Griffith, who had gone to the rue de la Planche for the latest news, reported later that he had found his country's representative standing in the midst of a group of wailing women and children in total disarray.

If anyone harbored hope that the monarchy's defenders would put a stop to their misguided efforts, the Duke of Brunswick's manifesto was the final straw. For all his liberal tendencies, this aristocratic Freemason who commanded the forces allied against France had foolishly signed a decree that proposed to restore the King and destroy the city of Paris. Instead of intimidating the Parisians, the Brunswick manifesto galvanized them. They needed no further proof that the King was in alliance with foreign powers intent on destroying the reforms wrought by the Revolution.

A number of American expatriates shared their indignation, among them Colonel David Humphreys, who had been appointed United States minister to Lisbon the year before. Humphreys' admiration for revolutionary France now redoubled. A frequent guest of Jefferson at the Hôtel de Langeac and of the Paris salons, Humphreys had literary pretensions. His "Ode to the Armies," written to fan his countrymen's ardor during their revolutionary war, had been translated by the Marquis de Chastellux and well received in Paris. To return the compliment, he translated Racine's *Athalie*, followed by Fabré d'Englantine's "Il pleut, il pleut, bergère," which the ingenuous author made known in America under the title "It rains, it rains, my fair."

Before the news of the regime's collapse had reached Lisbon, Humphreys wrote to Morris, outlining a plan that he thought might fatally weaken the Austrian and Prussian armies before they reached France: to wit, that the invading armies be encouraged to desert by distributing a proclamation in German that offered them passage to the United States at French expense. The proclamation should contrast

> the hardship of their situation . . . with the benefits they will enjoy in becoming free Citizens of the U.S. They might be told the numbers of Germans who chose to remain in America after the last war . . . [and] how many of their countrymen . . . are now happy, independent and rich in Pennsylvania and other parts of the U.S.

To this letter, Humphreys added messages for Lafayette and La Rochefoucauld, informing them of his plan. To Morris he added in closing: "You are now in a Theatre of the most important action that can easily be conceived. Everything seems hastening to a Crisis. Every post, every packet, every moment we expect to hear of great events."

His letter impressed on Morris the depth of his countrymen's enthusiasm for the French Revolution. Although Morris took this to heart, he also wondered how America would take the news of the collapse of the constitutional monarchy and the flight of their beloved Lafayette.* Morris was having his own difficulties: because of the distance between Paris and Philadelphia, his directives were out of date when they arrived, and he was forced to devise his own policy. Of one thing he was certain: his diplomatic colleagues might pack their bags but he was not going to follow their example, for he was determined to remain behind. In spite of his many faults, Morris was a man of character.

The reverberations from Humphreys' letter reached Morris a few days later in the person of a Bostonian named Thomas Hinchman who called on his arrival from London. According to his visitor, the events of August 10 had caused such alarm in the British capital that he had not dared bring the mail pouch the American minister in London wanted him to transmit to Morris. Hinchman had fully expected to find the country smoldering in ruins and was certain he would be searched. To his great surprise, he was warmly welcomed by a calm and courteous population. As if that were not enough, he couldn't heap enough praise on the excellent hotel where he was staying in Paris.

Hinchman gave his hearty approval to Morris' decision to stick to his post. As early as August 21, the American minister had written to Lebrun-Tondu, the churchman turned revolutionary who was now in charge of foreign affairs, to inform him that he was remaining in Paris. Hinchman made Morris swear that he would not consider leaving without a compelling reason, saying he would otherwise be judged very harshly in the United States.

By the beginning of September, the blind fury unleashed

* In protest against the Paris insurrection, Lafayette had surrendered himself to the foreign alliance.

by the terror* was carrying off several friends of America. As a result, Gouverneur Morris, who was not given to sentimentality, had to spend his precious time writing letters of condolence. To the Duchesse d'Orléans, he expressed his sorrow at the death of her sister-in-law, the Princesse de Lamballe. Next he wrote to William Short in The Hague to inform him of the death of Charles de Rohan-Chabot, Rosalie's much loved brother, and—almost casually—of her husband's assassination a few days later.

> I do not go into a recital of what has lately pass'd here. It is too shocking, and among the victims are some whose fate will much affect you. Poor Charles Chabot is no more. . . . Among the many scenes of bloodshed which have of late been exhibited you will lament the fate of the duke de La Rochefoucauld, kill'd in the presence of his aged mother. Knowing how much you interest yourself in the fate of this worthy family I feel obliged to tell these unhappy tidings.

To spare his feelings, Morris did not tell Short that the young duchess had been with the "aged mother," watching her own husband's murder. This Short learned from the duke's cousin, Alexandre de Liancourt, who wrote him that "M. de La Rochefoucauld was killed at Gisors. He was in the carriage, with his mother, his wife, and Mme. d'Astorg. The three ladies are well, thus do not be alarmed. You can picture their grief. . . . Do not be worried, for she is in no danger." At the same time, news reached Short of Lafayette's flight and subsequent arrest. Tragedy was surrounding him on all sides.

---

* The anarchy that began on August 10 reached a fevered pitch on September 2 as Paris learned of the successes of its enemies at Verdun. This touched off a bloody massacre of royalists that continued for almost a week. Bloody as it was, it did not compare to the Reign of Terror under the Committee of Public Safety a year later.

Short was now assailed by doubts: should he profit from the misfortune to his beloved, widowed under the most horrible circumstances, and try to win her hand? Could he ignore Lafayette and leave him to his fate when the road to the scaffold passed under Short's very window?

Lafayette's flight marked the final collapse of his policies. Five days after the imprisonment of the royal family in the Temple, he had urged his troops to renew their vows to the nation, to the law, and to the captive sovereign. The army proved hostile to his suggestion, and Lafayette became embittered. His failure weighed heavily on him. Though other officers of noble blood had seen fit to retain their commands and stand guard at the frontiers, the knight-errant of the constitutional monarchy did not see how he could follow their example. Already charges had been raised against him in the National Assembly. The time had obviously come to abandon camp and cross enemy lines in the hope of reaching the coast, and from there the United States.

Promptly arrested and imprisoned by the foreign allies, Lafayette sought a way out of his predicament and immediately thought of William Short, little Short who used to hover in Jefferson's shadow in the Hôtel de Langeac. Lafayette had wanted him, rather than Morris, named United States representative in Paris, but now, as minister to The Hague, Short was virtually next door to Lafayette's prison. The marquis picked up his pen:

Nivelle, August 26

Dear Friend,

You have heard of the dreadful events of August 10, when the Jacobin faction overthrew the constitution and had the King and the Assembly at their mercy. The army has abandoned me, and I have no choice but to leave France. We were arrested en route by a detachment from the Austrian army, in violation of international law, as cited in the enclosed declaration which I beg you to have published.

Then the marquis came to the point:

You would be rendering me a great service if you would go to Brussels as soon as you receive this note and insist that you see me. I am an American citizen who has left the service of France. You will be within your rights, and I trust you will come as soon as possible. God bless you.

Given his predicament, the marquis may have thought his claims well grounded. Short knew, however, that his claim to immunity as an American citizen would be declared a joke by Brunswick's army. For Short, the matter was made worse by the fact that the United States, which was doing its best to steer clear of troubled European waters, was not likely to recognize as its own a French aristocrat so notably associated with the French Revolution since its very inception. Even worse, without formal instructions from his government, how could Short intervene with the Emperor and the King of Prussia—especially as the United States had representatives in neither Vienna nor Berlin?

Although there was no question of his going to Brussels, Short's conscience troubled him nonetheless. It was an unkind fate indeed that obliged him to ignore Lafayette's call for help and to do nothing while the marquis was being carried off by the turbulent current of history.

The French government was not taken in by Morris' letter to Lebrun-Tondu announcing that he would stay at his post. Morris' good faith seemed of doubtful quality, compared to that of proven friends like Thomas Paine and Joel Barlow. For the time being, however, the French government had no choice but to deal with the American minister on the problem of Lafayette. And since Lebrun, and especially Clavière, who was now in charge of collecting taxes, were in dire need of funds, the Treasury needed the American diplomat. They had various financial transactions under consideration that might well replenish the nation's coffers. For one, the United States was committed to pay three million florins borrowed in Antwerp to the French representative in Philadelphia, a sum urgently needed to defray expenses in the Caribbean. For another, a payment of six million francs of the American debt to France had fallen due at the beginning of August, and the American government had arranged a loan from the Dutch bankers to meet this obligation.

Gouverneur Morris was no more than a go-between for these two operations, for even though William Short was now in The Hague, he remained in charge of financial arrangements with France, and it was he who held the key to the coffers in Antwerp and Amsterdam. His letter informing the French government that he was now in a position to pay the American debt arrived just as the monarchy was collapsing. Since no legally constituted authority had as yet replaced the King, Short and Morris agreed that the suspension of royal power meant the suspension of payments as well. Faced with this vacuum, Short retreated into his shell to await developments.

The French ministers protested vehemently over the Americans' casuistry. According to them, the debt was not due "the King" but "the Nation," and the phrase in the official documents mentioning payments to "his most Christian Majesty" was a stylistic convention now null and void. To find a way out of the dilemma, Lebrun-Tondu and Clavière joined forces with Monge, the Minister of the Navy, and invited Morris to meet with them at the Foreign Ministry on August 28.

After hearing them out, Morris tried to gain time by declaring that his government had not yet authorized him to do business with the new regime. He would have to ask Philadelphia for instructions. At a time when events were moving so much faster than the mails, the French ministers found his excuse preposterous. Tempers flared and they parted on chilly terms.

The next day, Lebrun wrote Morris, underscoring the suffering that the lack of funds was causing in the Caribbean. After delivering this alarm, he then baldly inquired: if, as Morris protested, he did not have the power to negotiate with them, what, pray, was his function? And he continued: "We have too high a regard for the friendship binding the United States to France to believe that the American representative could or should, on any pretext whatsoever, hesitate to bring to fruition an arrangement instigated by M. Short whose successful conclusion has been entrusted to your care." Lebrun then added: "The King is but suspended, and since moreover the government itself has not and will not change, no representative may refuse to negotiate with it, without the express orders of his court or its agents." This being the case, Lebrun repeated his demand that the United States meet its obligation to release the 800,000 "dollards" that Short had placed at France's disposal.

Morris immediately wrote Lebrun to inform him that he found his tone unacceptable: "The style of your letter of August 30 forces me to ask for a passport to leave France. I

136

shall travel with my own horses by easy stages and take the route to England by way of Calais. I leave behind my house, secretary, and a certain number of my servants pending instructions from the United States."

Lebrun backed down quickly. "You failed to catch the meaning behind certain expressions. . . . You should have understood, Monsieur, that you would have found us more than eager to give you satisfaction on any and all points based on reason and justice." He then proceeded to invoke, with considerable adroitness, the role that Benjamin Franklin had played in Paris "before the separation of your country from England." At that time, France had recognized American envoys in spite of their uncertain status and had signed a treaty with America despite the absence of any recognized government. In addition, his country had sent an envoy to Congress when the Americans were still subjects of the King of England and their country a British colony. In closing, Lebrun asked Gouverneur Morris not to leave France without further reflection and expressed the hope that he would reverse his decision. In the meantime, however, he ordered Morris' passport.

Mollified, the American minister replied: "I have recovered my determination to remain in France and await the orders of my court." If there was a touch of malice in his reference to the American Cabinet as "my court," the provocation went unnoticed.


While the French armies were fighting on its frontiers, the National Assembly ordered elections for representatives to the National Convention that was to replace it. Four different *Départements*—Oise, Aisne, Pas-de-Calais, and Puyde-Dôme—elected Thomas Paine as their deputy.* Two British travelers, Lord Lauderdale and Dr. John Moore, stopping at an inn in Abbeville, overheard local citizens declare that they too had considered choosing Paine as deputy from their *Département*, the Somme. Such was the popularity of an American who had never set foot in the French provinces, who was in England at the time, and who, unable to speak a word of French, had had to communicate with his electorate through an interpreter.

Paine would have found it difficult to choose among the four *Départements* had not Achille Audibert, a distinguished citizen of Calais, taken the first boat to England to convince Paine to represent his *Département*, where he would find himself in the company of Carnot, Lebas, and Robespierre. Paine let himself be persuaded, to the dismay of the other districts. Bancal des Issarts, thinking him won over to the Auvergne, had already addressed him a letter from Clermont-Ferrand: "Come, friend of man, and swell the ranks of the patriots in an assembly which will determine the destiny of a great people and perhaps even that of the whole human race. The era of happiness you predicted for the nations of the world has arrived."

Another letter, no less enthusiastic, came from Hérault de Séchelles, president of the Assembly about to be dissolved:

France calls you to her breast, Monsieur, to fill the most useful and therefore the most honorable of functions: to bring about, through sound legislation, the happiness of a people whose destiny concerns all those who think and suffer in this world. It is only natural that the nation which has proclaimed the

* Ironically, the man who was so often deemed a dangerous radical took his seat with the Girondists on the right side of the legislative chambers.

"Rights of Man" should wish to include among its lawmakers the man who first gave voice to these principles in his book, *Common Sense*, a work which takes its inspiration from nature and the society of men.

In England, Paine's election caused such a scandal that the new deputy began to fear for his safety. To be sure of getting his man to Calais unharmed, Achille Audibert dogged his every footstep. One night, while they were dining with several British "Jacobins," an officer came in to warn them that the police were looking for Paine, and that if he wanted to avoid a trap, he would do well not to go home that night.

William Blake, always quick to move into the breach, helped Paine plan his clandestine departure for France. Audibert and the lawyer John Frost—another revolutionary fanatic—went with him. When the three men disembarked at Calais, they were welcomed with waving flags and cheers. Spurned in England, Paine was received with open arms in France.

True to his promise to Thomas Pinckney, now American minister in London, Paine went to see Gouverneur Morris the very day he arrived in Paris and handed him the letters Pinckney had entrusted to his care—the same letters that the faint-hearted Hinchman had been too nervous to deliver the month before. These letters concerned the fate of Lafayette (whom Pinckney scrupulously avoided mentioning by name) and the marquis's desire to have America's representatives in Europe claim him as an American citizen. Pinckney took a dim view of the idea and wanted to know what Morris thought. Writing in response, Morris stated that he feared they would do the cause more harm than good, and that moreover, it was already too late for the American ministers in Paris, London, and The Hague to mount a concerted effort on the marquis's behalf: Morris knew for certain that "the person" had left for an unknown destination and was already far away. Morris also informed Pinckney that on the day following his visit to the Paris legation, Paine had taken his seat at the Convention and had voted with the majority for the abolition of royalty in France.

Paine's electoral triumph went to the heads of his London friends. Joel Barlow, convinced that his time had come, expressed his deepest convictions in an "Address to the National Convention." Abbé Grégoire was presiding the day that Paine brought Barlow's plan for a new constitution to the deputies' attention. The abbé's homage to Barlow was echoed by Brissot, who praised the plan in his newssheet *Le Patriote français*. As Abbé Grégoire had done already, Brissot proposed that the author be honored with French citizenship for his work, which he deemed second only to Paine's "Rights of Man." Dr. John Warner, former chaplain at the British embassy in Paris, wrote Barlow to congratulate him on the reception given his suggestions and to affirm with enthusiasm that "France is remaking the world."

The British government, justifiably nervous, considered Barlow to be every bit as dangerous as Paine. For some time, Barlow had been doggedly translating texts by Brissot and Clavière in order to familiarize the British with revolutionary principles. In quick succession, he had published "A Warning to the Privileged Orders" and a brochure entitled "The Conspiracy of Kings." Now, the Convention ordered the publication of an English version of Barlow's "Letter to the National Convention in France on the Vices of the Constitution of 1791 and the Extent of the Remedies to Be Applied" for consumption in Britain. The British government had had enough, and Barlow sensed that the moment had come to leave for France.

The victories of the French armies at Valmy and Jemmapes gave the British liberals renewed faith in the French Revolution. The forces of liberty and the enemies of kings shouted their encouragement across the Channel, and the Constitutional Society of London organized a delegation, headed by Joel Barlow and John Frost, to present its personal congratulations to the Convention for the recent victories in the field.

While the delegation was making its way to France, a group of English patriots living in Paris joined forces with their French friends to organize a victory celebration. The festive reunion took place at the Hôtel White near the church of Notre-Dame-des-Victoires, an establishment run by a British subject. The party included several members of the Convention brought by Thomas Paine. John Stone, a disciple of Joseph Priestley and Dr. Richard Price, presided over the banquet. Stone had recently founded an association called Friends of the Revolution in England to honor the memory of Oliver Cromwell as well as the republicans and regicides who were his disciples.

Obviously, Gouverneur Morris was not among those invited. The victory of the rabble over the disciplined armies of the King left him cold, and his loathing for the democrats grew day by day. If he had heard Joel Barlow call the members of the Convention "benefactors of humanity," his horror would have known no bounds.

Despite Morris, Franco-American friendship was at fever pitch, and, warmed by wine, the guests at the Hôtel White raised their glasses to toast the patriotic societies of Britain and Ireland and to drink to the health of friends present and absent. The names of Fox and Sheridan, Dr. Priestley and Mackintosh, Thomas Cooper and Horne Tooke were invoked, along with the British parliamentarians sympathetic to the Revolution and members of the Convention. Carried away by the spirit of the occasion, Sir Robert Smyth and young Lord Edward Fitzgerald rose to proclaim, with a fervor worthy of the night of August 4,* that they were giving up all titles and privileges. Then John Stone and the same young Fitzgerald proposed that a "British Club" be founded in Paris to keep alive the spirit of unity that had animated them this night.

The following week, two different English-speaking groups presented themselves at the bar of the Assembly. The ushers guiding them were still in court dress, so quick had been the transition from the King's service to the Nation's. First came the English, Scots, and Irish residing in Paris. Like dancers in a carefully choreographed ballet, they entered, marched single file to the bar, regrouped, bowed, and made their speech:

> Citizen legislators.
>
> The Irish and British citizens currently in Paris assembled on Sunday, November 18, to celebrate your armies' brilliant successes and unanimously decided that they owed the representatives of such a great nation the tribute of their congratulations.

The reception given this little speech and Abbé Grégoire's response charmed the delegates, who blissfully drank in the compliments showered on them from all sides. Next came the

---

* August 4, 1789, the night on which the Assembly decreed the abolition of privilege—in effect, an end to the feudal system. Impassioned nobles and clergymen rose one after the other on that night to renounce the vested rights they had held.

delegates from the Constitutional Society of London led by Joel Barlow and John Frost. They in turn addressed themselves to the "citizens of France" by way of the Convention, and pressed them to continue their efforts to promote the happiness of mankind. Then their spokesman rose to still greater heights:

> Like the faint glimmerings of an aurora borealis, the spark of liberty, nurtured in England during the course of several centuries, served only to reveal to the rest of Europe the total obscurity in which it lay. A more intense light, similar to that of the true dawn, blazed forth from the heart of the American Republic, but at too great a distance to illuminate our hemisphere. It was not until—if the limpidity of your language will allow me to complete the metaphor—as I was saying, it was not until the French Revolution, shining with all the intensity of the sun at its zenith, revealed the practical results of that philosophy whose principles had been sown in the dark. Everywhere, its influence is dispelling the clouds.

The address concluded on a more prosaic note: "The society we represent has sent one thousand pairs of shoes as a patriotic gift to the soldiers of liberty; these shoes have already arrived in Calais." Another thousand pairs were to follow, a gesture all the more touching as winter was fast approaching.

In response, Abbé Grégoire gave his usual silver-tongued reply. Expressing the nation's thanks both for the kind words and for the shoes, he described the British delegates as "proud children of a nation that has brought fame to two worlds." At the conclusion of the meeting, it was decided to send the texts of the day's speeches to the national printing house so that they could be immortalized in a brochure published "by order of the Convention."

The Anglo-Saxons were so impressed by the setting, the heroic atmosphere, and the embraces that they failed to realize that effusive speeches and scenes like these were a daily occurrence at the Convention. To the deputies and tribunes, the presence of these foreigners at the bar was all part of a familiar ritual. Their genius lay in keeping the tone at a fever pitch; by renewing it each day, every man present was deluded into thinking that the session he had just witnessed was exceptional, a day that would go down in the annals of revolutionary history.

Aside from the fact that he had been identified in the French newspapers as an Englishman—a mistake he quickly rectified—Joel Barlow had every reason to congratulate himself on his stay: the French capital had smiled on him, the Scioto disaster was forgotten. He and Paris had made a fresh start, and both were getting carried away by the current of the new ideas; to both, the prospect of a golden age seemed not only imminent but the most natural thing in the world.

Joel had but one regret: Thomas Paine's ignorance of French had reduced him to silence in the Convention. What a pity that America could not make itself heard by a voice that carried such authority! Meanwhile, Barlow was making new friends who caused him to feel ever closer to France, and his hopes rose even higher when he heard that he was about to be named a French citizen. If this could happen, why shouldn't the door of the Convention one day open for him?

Opportunity soon struck. General Montesquiou's republican army had just conquered the Kingdom of Savoy. To a man, the Savoyards spontaneously broke the chains that bound them to their king and nobility and asked to join France. On the heels of the English and American delegations, representatives from Savoy appeared at the bar of the

144

Convention to communicate their countrymen's desire to become French citizens. With the fraternal blessing of Abbé Grégoire, their request was forwarded to the Diplomatic and Constitutional Committees, which gave it a warm welcome. Abbé Grégoire was asked to write a report on the incorporation of this new territory, and it was not long before Hérault de Séchelles announced from the tribune that Savoy had been united with France. The Convention immediately directed that Hérault, together with Abbé Grégoire and two other deputies, go to Chambéry and organize the new *Département*, thenceforth to be known as "Mont-Blanc."

Abbé Grégoire was high on the list of Barlow's Paris friends. The abbé's personality, his liberal views, his love of art and literature, as well as his endearingly old-fashioned manners, had won the American over. During the course of a conversation, the subject of the imminent elections in Savoy arose, and Abbé Grégoire gave Joel to understand that his candidacy to the post of representative for Mont-Blanc would be looked upon with favor. The churchman invited Joel to accompany the Convention delegation to Savoy.

As a result, Joel had to write Ruth in December that instead of returning to London, he was off to the mountains, and begged her to be patient.

Having gone to Paris to drink at the fountain of Liberty, Joel now found himself deep in the *Département* of Mont-Blanc among a people intoxicated with their new independence. And, as he wrote to Ruth, he himself had been welcomed "with fraternity and respect."

As soon as they arrived in Chambéry, the commissioners quickly disbanded the local senate and former administration, although out of necessity, Abbé Grégoire had to keep the old administrative machinery, which he qualified as "provisional." While waiting for the new elections, he celebrated mass in Chambéry cathedral with the local bishop's permission.

Meanwhile, Joel Barlow was testing local opinion, and since the electoral situation seemed favorable, he decided to try his luck at becoming the second American deputy at the Convention. Under the mantle of the four commissioners from Paris, he made contacts with his future constituents, learned the history of the Allobroges (the ancient Gallic tribe whose very name had been unknown to him three weeks before), and acquainted himself with the needs and aspirations of the population.

Although Barlow found the Savoyards to be "a people, vigorous and hardy, just born to liberty," he was not content to conquer only them. A man of irrepressible enthusiasm, Barlow was already looking beyond the boundaries of his future constituency. For ten days he labored at composing "A Letter to the People of Piedmont on the Advantages of the French Revolution and the Necessity of Adopting Its Principles in Italy." In this pamphlet, printed in Grenoble in both French and Italian and distributed by the republican authorities, Barlow sought to entice the Piedmontese away from their Sardinian ruler and induce them to join the Savoyards under the banner of Liberty—in other words, France. Giving their fantasies full rein, patriots like Barlow were beginning to envisage a republic of limitless frontiers.

Regional politics were forgotten whenever Barlow and his colleagues received letters and newspapers from Paris. Louis XVI's trial was under way, and they discussed at length the rumors concerning the King's fate. Ever since Varennes, Abbé Grégoire had maintained that the King's flight was an opportunity "furnished by Providence to establish a Republic," and as early as November he had declared himself in favor of a trial. As for the verdict, he thought banishment was enough. "All I want is that the guilty be rendered harmless." He rejected with horror the idea of an execution—"a hangover from barbarian times"—and so eloquent was he on this subject that when it came time to write to the Convention making known their opinion, all four commissioners spoke against the death penalty.

In the quiet of his furnished room, Joel Barlow sought relief from these somber questions at his writing desk. One day his hostess served him a cake that reminded him so much of a certain New England delicacy that he dashed off an ode in three cantos to its glory. Many critics consider Barlow's *The Hasty Pudding* to be his happiest venture into poetry. During this period he also wrote regularly to his wife—informative, bantering letters laced with expressions of love and devotion. He spoke at length of the proud Allobroges and avoided—for Ruth's sake—any mention of the Savoyard ladies, the public balls at which the people danced with such republican abandon, or the Comtesse de Bellegarde and her sister, who delighted all eyes as they twirled to the strains of revolutionary airs in their white gowns adorned with cockades and tricolored ribbons. The Comte de Bellegarde had emigrated to Turin, where he was brandishing his sword in the service of the King.

Unfortunately for her virtue, dancing in public places was not enough for Mme. de Bellegarde: in addition, she spent her nights enchanting Commissioner Hérault de Séchelles, who was a handsome man of thirty-three, the son of an officer in the King's army, and one of Marie Antoinette's protégés before the Revolution.

147

Of all this Joel said not a word to Ruth, confining himself to the delights of matrimony and the bright prospect of their imminent reunion in Paris. From foggy England, Ruth—who always seemed on the verge of tears—lamented: "Would to Heaven you had not left me." She reproached him for his association with John Frost, saying he should never have gone to Paris with him, that Frost's reputation was so bad in London it had besmirched his own. "Here you cannot return at present. Every thing evil is said of you, & I am obliged to avoid company not to hear you abused." She kept repeating: "You cant return safely. . . . Your affairs here are completely ruined."

If the British newspapers were speaking ill of him, Joel could have the satisfaction of knowing that Edmund Burke had spoken "honorably" of him on the floor of Parliament, referring to him as "Prophet Joel." But as Ruth was certain that their correspondence was being read by the British "black cabinet," he should henceforth send his letters in a double envelope, the outside envelope addressed to Mark Leavenworth, an American merchant in England on business at the time whom the police had no reason to suspect.

In her loneliness, Ruth had a tendency to make mountains out of molehills, and she did not relish the idea of Paris at all. If Joel insisted she join him in France, let it be Boulogne-sur-Mer, where they could more easily embark for the United States. Among her forebodings, she feared an imminent war between England and France. What would happen to them if hostilities broke out and all the ports were closed? She already felt the trap closing in on her.

Perhaps to Ruth's relief, the Allobrogian voters did not choose to elect Joel Barlow, and the disappointed candidate returned to Paris. There he installed himself at the Hôtel

White, which had become the Maison de Philadelphie—the words *hôtel* (a noble residence) and "White" (the traditional color of the royalists) having an unfortunate ring in 1793. To make up for his lost electoral battle, France honored Barlow with French citizenship, and Abbé Grégoire, calling him "my dear fellow-citizen," wrote him: "If the voters of Mont-Blanc had been looking after their own best interests, that is to say, the interests of the country, you would now be occupying a seat in the legislature."

Ruth continued to write Joel from London, begging him to return to the United States with her. Still undecided, he turned a deaf ear to her entreaties, and as soon as he found suitable lodgings in the Palais Egalité (the former Palais Royal), he called her to his side. He told her that there were about to be important changes in his life; he had "new plans" that involved new and unexpected occupations. Poor Ruth would have died of fright had she known what he had in mind. Looking beyond the region of the Scioto, Barlow's eyes had come to rest on Louisiana.

# III
# FRANCE
# UNDER
# THE REPUBLIC:
# 1793–1794

# 7

THE TREATY SIGNED BY THE UNITED STATES AND ENGLAND IN 1783 had cooled relations between France and the United States. Louis XVI's Foreign Minister, Vergennes, resented the treaty, and the French court was left with a bitter taste in its mouth. Was this their reward for playing the Good Samaritan to the American colonies? As if this were not enough, the American war had increased the disorder in French finances and the already considerable confusion in men's minds. The only good that had come of it was the minor satisfaction of seeing the British monarchy lose face.

Meanwhile, victorious and free, the United States moved serenely in Britain's economic and spiritual sphere. It was only when revolutionary France began to feel its oats that it thought itself capable of tearing its ally from Britain's grasp. According to the republicans, the lull in Franco-American friendship was caused by negligence on the part of the Ancien Régime. Quite early, the National Convention envisaged a "new alliance between the French and American Republics" that would contribute to Jefferson's dream of "the union of the two hemispheres."

Alas, the new government* was soon bogged down in the same policy that had hobbled Louis XVI. The dying monarchy had already been amply warned by Louis's last minister to the United States, the Chevalier de Ternant. The new republic would have done well to consider the reports of this farsighted diplomat, but it preferred to cling to its illusions; the realities of the American situation remained as obscure to the new government as they had to the old.

But the astute Talleyrand was not taken in. Having fled to the United States to avoid the vicissitudes of the Revolution, he was to write: "America is nonetheless wholly English, in the sense that England has every advantage over France when it comes to deriving the benefits that one nation can derive from another. I maintain therefore that it is to England, far more than to France, that the United States wants to be and will be of greater use."

American business activities, domestic life, traditions, and prejudices all followed the British model; even God spoke English, and America's children learned to read the King James version of the Bible. Their basic instincts drew them to the English; the French always tended to baffle them. By the same token, the French had difficulty understanding the American cast of mind. What Frenchman would ever have taken up arms against royal authority over a tax on tea? Paradoxically, the English were far from popular in the United States, while Americans continued to have a soft spot

---

* In August, Danton had called for elections to a National Convention which was to replace the Assembly. Among its tasks were deciding the fate of the King and drafting a new constitution to supersede the previous one that had established a constitutional monarchy. The new Convention assembled on September 20, 1792; it was to continue its work for three years.

154

in their hearts for the nation that had sent its armies to their aid.

But business was business, and tender sentiments were of small account in the marketplace. The French could hardly hope to elbow the British from their position of preeminence in American trade. The Convention was nonetheless determined to try, with the aid of a treaty drawn up in due and proper form. All that was needed was an artful diplomat who could open the way to a rapprochement and lead negotiations to a successful conclusion. Brissot, the Convention's specialist in American affairs, found this rare bird in the person of Edmond Charles Genêt, recently returned to France after serving in the French embassy in Russia.

Genêt, not yet thirty, was the son of a bourgeois family formerly in the service of the court. During Vergennes's heyday, Genêt's father, then head of a bureau in the Foreign Ministry, had developed a passion for America. With an eye to his son's future, he had pressed the boy on the American merchants in Paris and especially on Benjamin Franklin. Franklin's house in Passy became a mecca for the fifteen-year-old. The American minister took a liking to the boy, and when Edmond Charles decided to improve his English in Nantes rather than Great Britain, Franklin gave him a letter of introduction to his nephew, then a merchant in Nantes, informing him that young Genêt had come to perfect his English because of the many Americans residing there.

When the boy had mastered the language, his father initiated him into the arts of diplomacy and found him minor posts with the French ambassadors in Berlin and Vienna. Genêt was only nineteen when his father died, and Vergennes let him fill his father's shoes at the Foreign Ministry before he moved on to posts with the embassies in London and St. Petersburg. Meanwhile Marie Antoinette took on two of his sisters as ladies-in-waiting, and the less pretty of the two married the son of a court flunkey.

Young Genêt seemed to fill all the requirements for the post in Philadelphia. The Girondists looked on him with favor, and Mme. Roland took him under her wing after a careful examination of his background and person. His nomination was approved by the Convention in November 1792, and the Executive Council drew up the instructions for his mission: "The republicans who have replaced the infamous lackeys of despotism hasten to mark out for Citizen Genêt a path diametrically opposed to the twisting byways down which his predecessors were made to crawl."

With these directives in hand, the diplomat was to negotiate a pact "based on more liberal and fraternal foundations" than the alliance of 1778. So much was clear, but underneath lay the veiled intentions of the Executive Council concerning, among other things, Louisiana.

If the icy reaches of Canada had never appealed to the popular imagination, Frenchmen had retained a certain nostalgia for hot and humid Louisiana ever since John Law, the Scottish banker who had briefly repaired France's ailing finances, launched his speculatory rocket. Even though Louisiana had been ceded to Britain and Spain by the Treaty of Paris,* the rocket's dazzling trail still hung in the revolutionary air. By giving aid to the American rebels, Louis XVI had avenged British wrongs to France, but at the same time this action also brought the New World back to

---

* Signed in 1763, the treaty ceded French territories east of the Mississippi to Great Britain and western Louisiana to Spain. It was not until 1800 that France, under Napoleon, regained the western section from Spain.

his subjects' minds. And instead of assuaging France for the loss of its American possessions, the King added insult to injury by sending French troops to regions originally discovered and conquered by the French. Vergennes, with his usual foresight, anticipated the day when France would retrieve those territories conquered by La Salle and colonized by his successors.

Following America's independence, Versailles watched with some satisfaction as Louisiana, Florida, and the Mississippi River became bones of contention between the young American republic and its Spanish neighbors. While maintaining an outward appearance of neutrality, the French let the situation worsen, waiting for the moment when they would be called in to settle the dispute.

Louisiana cast the same spell on the revolutionary regime as it had on the Bourbons, and France's new leaders were fated to follow in the footsteps of the monarchy in their efforts to revive a dead past. Thus the plebeian Executive Council took up the matter of Louisiana for its own ends, but in the same spirit as the monarchy before it. To allay their consciences, however, the Convention ingeniously disguised the Ancien Régime's threadbare policy by dressing it up in revolutionary colors. Since France was dedicating itself to the liberation of its neighbors from tyranny, and since her armies' victories during the autumn justified high hopes, why should Louisiana not be included in this crusade for liberty? With the Allobroges and the Belgians liberated, and the Batavians, Rhinelanders, and Helvetians about to be, how could France refuse to lend a helping hand to a former colony taken by force and still French by tradition, a colony that was begging to be delivered from the Spanish yoke?

First, the Americans must be dealt into the game; they

157

would be only too glad to help France rid Louisiana of the Spanish and, at long last, see their southern border redrawn to permit them free navigation on the Mississippi. This the French would guarantee in advance, while continuing to move the American pawn against the Spanish.

When Dumouriez took over the Ministry of Foreign Affairs, the thought of Louisiana enchanted him no less than it had Vergennes. The new minister quickly made contact with a group of battle-scarred veterans scheming in the cafés of the Palais Egalité and presented them with a plan. The idea, he explained, was not to recapture Louisiana by military force but to foment local disorders and thus ease the territory toward independence under a French protectorate.

One of these would-be troublemakers was Jean-Benoît Beaupoil, the man who had closed John Paul Jones's eyes the year before. Anxious to improve his standing as a *sans-culotte,* Beaupoil had divested himself of the awkward title of Comte de Saint-Aulaire. His accomplices, Pierre Lyonnet and a Portuguese named Pereira, were no less eager to foment a revolution in New Orleans.

Dumouriez turned over his portfolio to Lebrun-Tondu and went off to rejoin his army. But the specter of Louisiana followed him to his camp, for fate had placed under his orders one General Don Francisco de Miranda, a Venezuelan and veteran of the American War of Independence who had volunteered his services to France at about the same time as John Skey Eustace. While he was fighting for France, Miranda made no secret of the fact that he was only waiting for the day when he could do battle on the American continent, never mind where as long as its purpose was to dislodge the Spanish. In another time and place, Miranda's notions would have appeared ludicrous, but to brave hearts in 1792 nothing seemed impossible, not even the doubtful prospect of liberating Spanish America.

Together, Dumouriez and Miranda pored over maps and retraced the frontiers of the New World, evoking Louisiana sunshine in Flanders mud. Thanks to its location, Louisiana would provide the key to Florida and Mexico and open the way to the Spanish territories that lay beyond. While Miranda indulged his fantasies, Dumouriez communicated his enthusiasm to Lebrun-Tondu. In a letter dated November 30, he described "General Miranda's superb project" and added: "It would be to France's advantage to use diversionary tactics in this area—without harming the Americans—in order to weaken the power of England and Spain." Lebrun passed the message along to the Executive Council, which carefully examined both it and the project submitted by the three adventurers Dumouriez had discovered while Foreign Minister.

Obviously, the grandiose plans of the Girondists, as well as those of Miranda and Dumouriez's agitators, would require assistance from men on the spot. At this point, as a member of the Convention, Thomas Paine entered the picture although he was hardly inclined to this kind of shady operation. Through a friend, Dr. James O'Fallon, who lived in Louisville, Kentucky, he made contact with General George Rogers Clark, an officer always ripe for new adventures and more than willing to draw his sword on France's behalf. Paine acted as liaison between the Executive Council and this luckless soldier, who soon had a plan of his own to present—but not without a few strings attached: yes, he was ready to organize and lead an expedition against Louisiana, but only if he were first given the rank of general in the French army. The ultimatum was forwarded to Paris by

French agents in the United States. By February 1793, Paine was able to inform Dr. O'Fallon that the Republic's Provisional Council was regarding Clark's proposal with a favorable eye.

The author of *Common Sense* had high hopes for the campaign. His only worry was that certain British and royalist sympathizers among American politicians would interfere and prevent Clark from recruiting officers and men. Meanwhile the ranks of the conspirators continued to grow. Before long, the trio of Beaupoil, Lyonnet, and Pereira had attracted a pair of Americans—two of those strange wanderers common to the eighteenth century. One was Stephen Sayre from Long Island, who had been knocking around Europe after a spell in the Tower of London. An inventive sort, he was always badgering European courts to finance schemes that appeared as remarkable to him as they seemed risky to his prospective clients. He was now in Europe on his honeymoon, having married a Jamaican heiress, and while waiting for the various sovereigns' responses, was trying to set up a tobacco factory in France. During his wanderings, he had run into Miranda, who had drawn his attention to the problems of the Spanish-American colonies and had easily captured his enthusiasm. Sayre was pleased though not surprised to learn that France had its eye on Louisiana. Always eager to escape the daily routine, he was enchanted at the prospect of helping organize a revolt in New Orleans.

During that same autumn, another American entered the scene, although no one quite knew from where. His name was Gilbert Imlay, a handsome, articulate, and enterprising veteran of the American war who was vacillating between business and politics. Soon Imlay also had his fingers in the

Louisiana plot, for although he had sought exile in Europe, America remained his promised land.

According to Imlay, the best way to become a free man was not to stay in France where freedom had to be won by the sword, but to leave and colonize Kentucky, his supposed birthplace. His familiarity with the region enabled him to publish a description of the western part of the United States, and he expressed himself as ready to sell land along the frontiers to would-be colonizers. There, he declared, settlers could live as they pleased and till the virgin soil without interference from the government. Unfortunately, this region blessed by the gods and generously watered by the Mississippi suffered from intolerable injustice: all progress in the region was hampered by the difficulty of sending ships down a river jealously guarded by the Spanish, who owned a portion of its course and its mouth in the Gulf of Mexico. As a result, New Orleans, where their goods would normally be unloaded, was closed to the merchants and farmers of Kentucky. Captain Imlay could often be heard fulminating against the Spanish in Paris cafés.

Imperturbable by nature, Imlay found nothing surprising in France's claims to Louisiana, and as his sympathies of the moment were with the French, he longed to see the Spanish brought to their knees.

Before leaving London, Imlay had received a letter of introduction to Brissot from the philosopher, scientist, and lawyer Thomas Cooper; through Brissot, he was able to make useful contacts. Being an American, Imlay maneuvered with confidence in revolutionary Paris. As soon as he had sniffed the wind, he took up his pen and wrote a *Memorandum on Louisiana* to convince the ministers on the Committee of Public Safety—which had assumed virtual dictatorship over French affairs—to undertake the operation. Since their own ambitions were already inclined in this direction, the ministers hardly needed encouragement.

The plot took a new turn when the French government directed Edmond Charles Genêt, the newly named minister to the United States, to set it in motion. As soon as he had presented his credentials to Philadelphia, Genêt was instructed to "propagate the principles of the French Revolution in Louisiana, Kentucky, and the other provinces bordering the United States." To make his task easier, the Executive Council authorized him to make any expenditures "necessary to the success of the project" and to distribute *louis d'or* right and left "for the cause of liberty and the people's deliverance."

Genêt's American mission included a second project as well. Louis XVI was still shut up in the Temple awaiting judgment. Once his case was decided, it would be wise to determine his fate as quickly as possible. A few hotheads in the Convention wanted his neck, but they were a minority; the others, the men in power and the majority of the deputies, preferred to see him disappear quietly, either to prison or exile. Most of the Girondists favored the latter solution—and what better place for the burdensome monarch to end his days in obscurity and far from intrigues than in France's sister republic, the United States? Genêt's departure would almost coincide with the end of the King's trial, and if the vote was for banishment, the new minister could immediately take the royal family in hand and install it in his frigate, the *Embuscade.* Thus they would all reach a safe haven together. While the *Embuscade* was being fitted out for the crossing, Beaupoil and his friends also asked for berths on board.

Thomas Paine thought it best to tell Gouverneur Morris what was afoot. Morris immediately wrote to Washington:

> I have not yet seen Mr. Genêt, but Mr. Payne is to introduce him to me. . . . In addition to what I have said respecting the King to Mr. Jefferson, it is well to mention to you that the majority have it in contemplation . . . to send him and his family to America, which Payne is to move for. He mentioned this to me in confidence.

For once, Thomas Paine and Gouverneur Morris were of the same mind: the King must be saved. There were many reasons why Genêt was the ideal person to guard the King and execute the verdict. He had virtually grown up in the royal seraglio and he retained the fine manners of the Ancien Régime; two of his sisters had been in Marie Antoinette's entourage. At the same time, he was a tried and true republican and a pillar of civic virtue. The appropriateness of the choice appealed to the Girondist mentality. It would lend a kind of democratic grandeur to the departure of the exiled King, whom decent people wanted to see removed from the scene but not humiliated. He would embark like the hero in a classic drama, and once he had arrived on the other side of the Atlantic, "American gratitude," as Morris wrote to Washington, "was expected to do the rest."

But the advocates of banishment soon found themselves overpowered by the extremists, in the clubs as well as in the Assembly. Certain observers wondered if the Girondists had not finally met their match, and it began to look as if the *Embuscade* would never have the honor of transporting the royal family to new horizons. Even so, Thomas Paine refused to be discouraged. Like Abbé Grégoire before him, the author of *Common Sense* was repelled by the idea of the King's execution: "Try to put kings where they can do no harm, but under no circumstances allow yourself the liberty of cutting off their heads."

As for Louis XVI, Paine thought it unjust to make the dullard pay for the crimes of ancestors who had died peacefully in their beds. Once the Bourbons had been pried from the throne, Paine argued, they should be caged, but in gilded cages. To get his point across while there was still time, Paine mounted a frontal attack on the partisans of the guillotine. By November 30 he had alerted the president of the Convention concerning his position, and because he could not speak French to the tribune, wrote "Thomas Paine's Opinion Concerning the Judgement of Louis XVI" and had a French translation of it distributed to his colleagues. In this text he pleaded with the members of the Convention to show "some compassion for the dethroned monarch, a man of narrow and feeble mind, and badly brought up like all his kind." He ended with the wish that the United States might be "the refuge and asylum for Louis Capet. There, forever protected from the miseries and crimes of royal life, he could learn from the constant exposure to public prosperity that the true system of government is not that of kings but of representation."

Then he appended:

I make this proposal as a citizen of the American republic, highly conscious of the debt of gratitude he owes to France. I make it also as a man who—although an enemy of kings—has not forgotten that they belong to the human race. And finally, I make it as a citizen of France, because I regard it as the best and most prudent measure that one could adopt.

The voting began on January 14, 1793. The following day, Bancal des Issarts read a new text from Paine's pen,

"Thomas Paine's Reasons for Sparing the Life of Louis XVI." From his seat at the top of the "Mountain" *—the most radical section of the Convention—Marat rose to interrupt: "I denounce this spokesman; I maintain that these are not Thomas Paine's opinions. It is not a faithful translation."

Paine mounted the tribune to refute Marat and inform him that he did indeed intend to vote for banishment. There could have been no doubt in the Jacobin's mind about the accuracy of the translation, for his English was every bit as good as his French. Born in Switzerland of a Sardinian father, Marat had a medical degree from the University of St. Andrews in Scotland and had practiced in London for several years before coming to France. His best works had been written in English, starting with his first book, *The Chains of Slavery*, which had only recently been published in a French translation.

Whether expressed in French or English, Paine's position was perfectly clear. The two men glared at each other across the chamber. In a sense, these two deputies taking each other's measure held the fate of the King of France in their hands; ironically neither of them had a drop of French blood in his veins. Paine was at a disadvantage, however, for his inability to speak French marked him as a foreigner, whereas Marat had adapted to his milieu, even to adding a "t" to the end of his name.

On this same day, Brissot published a letter in his newspaper under the title *Louis-le-dernier* ("Louis the Last"), in which he also advocated sending the fallen monarch to the United States. To buttress his argument, Brissot cited Paine,

---

* The Jacobins were also known as the "Montagnards"—because most of their seats in the Convention were located in the highest section.

"who had learned in England that it is not by the death of one king that you rid yourself of all kings." But it was too late: by a vote of 387 to 334, the Convention voted that the King must die.

Paine, however, would not let the matter rest. On January 19, his last plea for clemency, "Should Louis XVI Be Spared?," was read before the Convention. Buzot, in an effort to gain time, spoke out in favor of a reprieve. Brissot supported him, saying that he feared a too precipitous execution of the sentence would lose the Revolution its English, Irish, and American friends. The roll call followed. When the name of Thomas Paine was called, Bancal des Issarts rose and replied that the deputy from Pas-de-Calais cast his vote for a stay of execution "in the name of his American brothers." But again it was too late. The King's fate was sealed; all that remained was to set the date.

The Convention's decision to send Louis XVI to the guillotine put an end to the project of transferring the royal family to the United States, thus depriving Genêt of his passengers. This being the case, the new minister hastened his departure. As he was about to embark, he received a note reading: "Mr. Morris has the honor of paying his compliments to M. Genêt and wishing him a bon voyage." To George Washington, Morris wrote in a somewhat different vein: "I have seen Mr. Genêt and he has dined with me. He has I think more of Genius than of Ability and you see in him at first Blush the Manner and Look of an Upstart."

When Genêt set sail, the Louisiana conspirators were left behind. There had been second thoughts at the Foreign Ministry, for no one wanted to take the responsibility for sending these mercenaries on a ship chartered for the Republic's official representative to the United States.

The most belligerent of the conspirators, Pierre Lyonnet, refused to give up. If only he had been able to see Lebrun-Tondu face to face, he could have persuaded him in an hour—or so he said in his petitions. But no, the minister had been too busy to receive him, and Lyonnet had had to state his case to underlings. Meanwhile, the hired toughs whom Lyonnet and his accomplices deemed necessary to take to America for their "great enterprise" were waiting, pending a decision from on high. Lyonnet sent forth a constant flow of letters and memoranda sounding the death knell of Spanish power in North America. First came his "Personal Considerations Concerning Louisiana," then "Removing Louisiana from the Spanish Yoke, with the Certitude of Success." The risks were few, he insisted: "This enterprise is not one of those demanding much money or many men. With a little financial backing, its success is assured, and France will have dealt a disastrous blow to Spain—without endangering a single head."

For all his efforts, Lyonnet was unable to produce a reaction in high places. Lebrun-Tondu took refuge behind the Committee of Public Safety, which had the final say in such matters. He pretended he was only a conduit for messages. But all appearances to the contrary, Lebrun was not inactive. Immediately after Genêt's departure, he submitted the various projects for Louisiana to the committee and asked for its approval to organize an expedition. In April he attacked Barère, a member of the committee, noting that this important dossier was gathering dust in the committee files. The matter must be taken up immediately, for—echoing Lyonnet's arguments—time was of the essence: they must take advantage of the season, autumn being the best time for launching military operations in that region. Why hesitate any longer, when France had such "easy means of execution" at its disposal? As far as he was concerned, he had good reason to be confident: "Every day I am solicited by those persons who first communicated these plans to me, and I deem myself capable of seeing that they prosper."

Having champed at the bit for months, "not daring to take up any kind of industrious activity" in order to be ready to leave for Louisiana at a moment's notice, Citizen Lyonnet finally despaired of ever reaching New Orleans and set out for Lyons instead. Perhaps that troubled city might offer him opportunities for "industrious activities" of a revolutionary sort. He had not quite given up hope, however, and kept up a running correspondence with Gilbert Imlay, who had been left in charge of the operation. Nor did he let Lebrun-Tondu's assistant, Guillaume Otto, forget him: "I would still like to know where things stand with the overseas operation. Citizen, please deign to remove me from this state of perplexity."

Imlay could not be bothered with the minister and his assistants; he went right to the Committee of Public Safety and proposed that he assemble a group of experts to organize the American expedition. One of these experts was none other than Joel Barlow. These, then, were the "new plans" he had mentioned to Ruth after his electoral rebuff! However, unlike his associates, Joel was hardly a swashbuckler and he risked little as a mere adviser on technical and revolutionary matters.

In the end, the Mississippi and Florida expedition never left Paris. Lebrun-Tondu and Barère were far too busy with the convulsions of French politics to spend their time looking for trouble overseas. By the end of April 1793, Dumouriez had deserted to the enemy, and Miranda, in disgrace after his defeat at Neerwinden, renounced his "superb project" forever.

Danton delivered the final blow from the Convention tribunal. This radical deputy did not believe in crusades, even when undertaken in the name of liberty and fraternity. After evoking a decree of the previous year that committed the Convention to help the oppressed overthrow their oppressors wherever they might be, he asked in tones heavy with sarcasm if France intended to help the Chinese, who were also in the throes of a revolution. "Let us decree," he ended, "that we shall in no way interfere with the affairs of our neighbors."

So much for the mirage of Louisiana. It continued to haunt a few dreamers, and the final gesture in favor of that territory's liberation came from Joel Barlow and Mark Leavenworth, with whom Barlow had associated himself in the effort. In December 1793, the two Americans submitted one last project to the Convention which, like its predecessors, was conceived with economy in mind: "How to Take Louisiana at No Cost to the Nation." The Convention, however, refused to rise to the bait. And there the matter rested.

On the day that Louis XVI's fate was sealed, a royalist took his revenge by mortally stabbing one of the regicides, Deputy Lepelletier de Saint-Fargeau, in a café near the Palais Egalité. And during a dinner in a nearby restaurant, Thomas Paine—who had voted against the death penalty—was set upon by a wild-eyed British officer. The good food and wine

169

had gone to Paine and Captain Grimstone's heads, the discussion had gotten out of hand, and all other arguments having failed, the captain resorted to insults: "Mr. Paine, you are an unworthy subject of His Majesty, an Englishman who has fought his own country at every opportunity, first in America, where you undermined the authority of the Crown, and then in France, where you continued to preach hatred of your native land. You are nothing but a traitor!"

A traitor! Paine replied with such heat that his opponent rushed at him and struck him in the face. The whole table rose to separate the two antagonists. At the word "police," Grimstone and his friends blanched. Any British soldier found guilty of assault on the person of a French deputy could find himself in a very nasty situation. And Paris judges would be even less inclined to clemency in Grimstone's case, for he had pitted his youth and strength against a man old enough to be his father.

Paine was the first to regain his composure. He refused to lodge a complaint and asked only that the young hothead take his belligerent ways back to England as fast as possible. He would even help him get a passport. The captain, completely sober by now, could hardly ask for more. But, unfortunately for Grimstone, the Palais Egalité, with its alluring *citoyennes* and gambling parlors, conspired to empty the pockets of adventurers from across the Channel. No matter how many times he counted his *assignats,* Grimstone could not come up with the price of his passage home. In a last gesture of generosity, Paine pulled a fat purse from his pocket, paid the balance, and turned on his heels.

When Captain Grimstone crossed the Channel in January 1793, George Schaffner had just made the trip in the opposite direction. The previous December, La Rouërie had sent his friend to London, a city then teeming with spies and counterspies. His mission was to take news of the Breton army and make known its urgent need for money and arms. At the same time, he was to find out how the counterrevolution was progressing, whether there were any projects for the following spring, and if so, when and where the landing would take place.

Schaffner returned to Brittany to find his comrade-in-arms secreted in a friend's manor and ill with fever. What had started as simple bronchitis threatened to bring the tempestuous hero's career to an inglorious end. Schaffner was so unnerved by the sight of the marquis wrapped in blankets in a remote house that he did not report the treachery that the émigrés in London had uncovered at the heart of the Breton conspiracy. A black sheep had contaminated the entire flock, and La Roüerie was its victim. Thus La Roüerie died—a week after the King's execution—without knowing that he had been betrayed by Dr. Chevetel, who had relayed to the King's enemies everything his former master had told him about the secret army.

La Roüerie's remains found a secret resting place in the garden of his hosts. Schaffner affixed his signature to the bottom of the document, sadly shouldered his gun, and disappeared. He had too many happy memories of rides across the Breton countryside with his friend to want to stay on, bitter and alone.

Across the Channel, with Chevetel's information to guide them, the republican authorities laid bare the machinations of the Breton conspiracy. The marquis's grave was discovered, the conspirators unmasked, and in June 1793 the trial began that would eventually lead them to the guillotine. But never once during these proceedings was George Schaffner's name mentioned. He was gone, never to return; historians who tried to pick up his trail assumed that he had been killed by the republicans, or died in the service of the princes' armies. But in fact, he had quietly gone to the Isle of Jersey, where he married and produced a son who later became a doctor on the medical faculty in Paris.

# 8

Two englishwomen in paris, helen maria williams and Mary Wollstonecraft, took the trial of Louis XVI very much to heart. When the moment came to vote the King's sentence, Miss Williams begged Bancal des Issarts, who was in love with her, to resist all pressure to vote for the guillotine. Although she was doubtless preaching to a convert, it pleased the man to let her think that his vote was dictated by her entreaties. As a result, Miss Williams boasted forever after about the one vote she had won from the wretched majority that condemned the King.

Mary Wollstonecraft happened to be living along the route to the guillotine. In a letter to her London editor, Joseph Johnson, she wrote:

> About 9 o'clock, this morning [January 21, 1793], the king passed by my window, moving silently along. . . . I can scarcely tell you why, but an association of ideas made the tears flow insensibly from my eyes, when I saw Louis sitting, with more dignity than I expected from his character, in a hackney coach, going to meet death, where so many of his race have triumphed!

173

Mary's tears dried when she met Gilbert Imlay at the home of Thomas Christie, another British pilgrim to the land of liberty who was living in Paris with his wife. Christie was Priestley's nephew and the author of *Letters on the French Revolution*, in which he refuted Burke and Calonne. He had met Mary through Johnson, their mutual friend and publisher.

If Imlay was first attracted by the physical charms of the red-haired feminist, he was soon no less fascinated by her lively mind. He himself had more than one arrow to his bow: a man of subtle imagination, he had written a novel to complement the brochure in which he described the territories to the west of the United States. *The Emigrants* combined the dream world of romance with the real world of financial speculation.

Mary and Imlay exchanged literary confidences. Doubtless the would-be seducer lavished praise on Mary's *Vindication of the Rights of Women* and the charming collection of stories that William Blake had illustrated. If literature was the immediate link, they soon found they also agreed on recent events in France, which they both saw as the harbinger of a golden age.

Less awkward than Bancal des Issarts with Miss Williams, Imlay rapidly found his way into his lady's good graces. At thirty, Mary was in full bloom. An expert in the art of feminine conquest, the American took the champion of women's rights completely by surprise. Yesterday's suitors— the painter Fuseli among them—seemed poor things compared to this Lothario from across the seas.

In order to devote themselves wholly to their idyll, the two lovers retreated to the woods at Neuilly, where a small cottage shielded them from public view. There, isolated from

174

the Paris of 1793, they would separate each morning. If unexpected business delayed Imlay's return or forced him to spend the night in Paris, Mary harried him with passionate notes. On his way home he would skirt the guillotine in the place de la Révolution and bring her the latest news and gazettes, along with his business papers. But Imlay was unable to arouse her interest in the world of speculation, even when he dangled the promise of future profits before her eyes. She translated into dreams what he translated into figures, and when the Convention began to tear itself apart, Mary saw it as the end of her illusions about popular representation, while Imlay avidly counted the profits that would accrue from civil disorder.

Mary spent the day at her desk. When evening came, she would go out into the garden and chat with their old gardener, who was not indifferent to her charms. When he saw her put on her shawl to go meet Imlay, he never failed to express his concern, for, to reach the city barrier, she had to cross the Bois de Boulogne, which was haunted by dangerous characters. Every evening he tried to discourage her from her foolhardy expedition, and every evening she would shake her head; the great love she had inspired made her immune to all dangers. Besides, far from being threatening, the Bois de Boulogne was dotted with bosky thickets that provided stopping places for the couple on their way home. When her daughter Fanny was born a few months later, Mary often referred to her as "the child of the barrier."

Before long, the sounds of civil strife inside the country and the boom of cannons on the nearby frontiers filtered into the prayer meetings of the Dunkirk Quakers. These friends of man found it difficult to adapt to the atmosphere of hatred, and as 1792 advanced, they became increasingly disturbed. To be sure, the Convention had reconfirmed the privileges accorded them by the Ancien Régime; their religious practices were not endangered. But all the same, the drums, the warlike chants, the flags, the pikes, the guns could not be pleasing to the Lord.

To these pure souls, the cult of the fatherland was no less scandalous than the cult of the Golden Calf. During the American Revolution they had kept their distance from both British and insurgents, for they recognized no kingdom other than the Kingdom of God. Now, in their view, the French had abandoned Papist tinsel and the accessories of Roman superstition only to burn incense to the Fatherland and festoon the trees of Liberty; they had replaced saints and relics with political idols, and far from returning to the Holy Bible, they were being led astray by examples from the heathen Plutarch instead. They indulged in a new fetishism, trading scapular for the red bonnet, and carrying busts of their profane heroes and replicas of the Bastille about in the streets. In their blindness, the French had simply exchanged one set of idols for another.

The hateful war was sure to spread: all signs pointed in that direction. Warships were rising from the waves like specters in a bad dream. Soon the sea, the gift of the Almighty to all his creatures, would become a moving battlefield, and once the war between France and England had broken out in earnest, the situation of the Nantucket whalers would become desperate.

Meanwhile their wives, in their severe hats and plain white aprons, walked the streets with downcast eyes and rapid steps. In the old days, sumptuary laws had kept the French people dressed in a state of relative decency, even in regions that harbored the despicable manufacture of lace. But with the abolition of these laws, lace was everywhere, even on the bonnets of the most humble citizens' wives, who with the coming of the Revolution had thrown all caution to the winds. Saddened by this spectacle, the Nantucket ladies agreed with their husbands that it was time to leave.

In the dead of winter 1793, a few ships left Dunkirk, now directly threatened by the war. Many a Nantucket whaler put his wife and children aboard and disappeared never to return. Even the patriarch William Rotch, once so eager to settle his people in France, took to the sea with his family. But the ways of the Lord are varied and mysterious, and some of the whalers chose to stay behind. Benjamin Hussey, the first Nantucketer to settle in France, continued to dispatch his three whaling ships under the command of hired captains, one of them his own son. For several more years, Nantucketers such as Jonathan Parker, Peter Brock, and Edward Starbuck could be seen, their black hats pulled down over their ears, on the wharfs of Dunkirk and Lorient.

Other sheep left the flock for good. The Nantucketers had attracted many a sea dog belonging to that international fraternity who, when asked where they came from, answered only: "I am a sailor." One of these was John Fleming, a Britisher who had married Alicia Church of Boston when she arrived in Dunkirk with the first whalers. While he was at sea, a member of the Rotch family who had elected to remain behind comforted the lonely young woman, and as soon as the new marriage laws went into effect in August 1793, Alicia asked for a divorce. History does not record what the Quaker matrons thought of Mrs. Fleming, who appears to have cast off the ritual bonnet and white apron. When the divorcée wed Francis Rotch, her marriage contract exposed the secrets of her wardrobe, which included a striped silk gown, a calico gown, an embroidered muslin gown, and a white satin gown, all of which the bride had brought to the community, not to mention multicolored stockings, dozens of muslin fichus, a blue satin fur-lined cloak, a tippet decorated with lace, and a fur muff of gray bear.

With his dear Ruth back at his side, Joel Barlow continued to rub elbows with politicians, businessmen, members of Convention committees, and merchant captains passing through Paris. At the same time he tried to make Ruth's life as agreeable as possible. She, in any event, was finding Paris much more to her liking than before. She was glad to see the Williams family again, as well as several of the ladies in the American colony. If most of them had remained true to character and were as she remembered them, the same could not be said of Mary Wollstonecraft. Gone were the days when she cried bitter tears at the thought of leaving the painter Fuseli in London, or at Louis XVI's cortège in Paris. She was now totally absorbed in her idyll with Imlay and was perfectly open about the nature of their relationship.

In New England, this couple would have caused a scandal, but one could hardly cross the ocean and disembark in the land of liberty with one's Puritan attitudes intact. The Yankee matrons in Paris treated the unlawful household as if it were quite legitimate. Under the shadow of the guillotine, the world was trembling on its foundations; in such conditions, why shouldn't these ladies—no less citizens than the rest—keep step with the times and adjust to revolutionary customs—at least during their stay in Paris? They would be back soon enough with the ancestral prejudices and the Salem and Marblehead grandmothers who saw no farther than the parish limits.

Besides, there were more pressing matters for concern. January had been a dreary month, followed by a chilly February, and March was no better. The war against England and Spain only added to the difficulties facing the country, and the problem of bread, already insoluble, was aggravated by the threat to shipping. As soon as war broke out between France and England, the British assumed the right to lay down the law and act as undisputed master of the sea. George III had even had the effrontery to forbid American ships to supply France and its colonies, and he also forbade them to take on supplies in the French colonies that were destined for France. At the same time, the British navy hunted down American ships, commandeered them, and laid claim to their cargoes. The United States responded by announcing it would take orders from no one. Incidents and recriminations followed, while Philadelphia lodged protest after protest with the Court of Saint James.

France was no less intransigent. When the English seized several cargoes of food destined for French consumption, it retaliated with a decree proclaiming: "French warships and privateers may henceforth intercept and bring into ports of the Republic all neutral vessels bearing in whole or in part provisions or merchandise belonging to the enemy."

As this measure did not spare the Americans either, it was in direct violation of the treaty of 1778. There was such a hue and cry among United States citizens in Paris and in the various French ports that a second decree was issued on May 23, tempering the language of the first. In accordance with a proposal of the Committee of Public Safety, the Assembly

179

decided that American ships would not be included in the provision of the first decree. Once again France was granting privileges to the ships and merchandise of her ally. Unfortunately, however, the continuing confusion made more measures necessary; the second decree was rescinded and, to make its intention crystal clear, the Committee of Public Safety, "desirous of maintaining the union established between the French Republic and the United States of America," had the Convention pass a decree on July 1, stating that the decree of May 9 in no way applied to American ships.

There the matter would have rested had French sailors not been capricious in their interpretations of their laws and regulations. American ships continued to be captured on the high seas and interned in French ports, and often the commercial tribunals called upon to litigate the cases judged these ships and their cargoes to be "lawful prizes." The Americans did everything in their power to regain possession of their goods and to collect damages, with interest.

Anxieties proliferated during the spring of 1793. The ill wind that had risen in France now blew straight across Europe. While republicans and royalists remained stubborn, Dumouriez vacillated between the two camps. The day came when he leaned too far in the wrong direction and arrested his friend Pierre de Beurnonville, the Minister of War, as well as the Convention delegates who had been chosen to bring him to his senses. He then turned them all over to the Austrians as hostages and defected to the enemy. Bancal des Issarts, a member of the delegation, was placed in captivity with the others. When, several years later, he finally saw Miss Williams again, he was still in love, but she had formed an alliance with John Stone.

Deep in Flanders mud, Dumouriez brought down several

followers with him in his fall, foremost among them the young Duc de Chartres, oldest son of Philippe Egalité.* The young duke fled to Switzerland in disguise, for his name was anathema everywhere and even a neutral country would have closed its doors to a member of that hated family.

The Americans in Dumouriez's army—General Eustace, Colonel Oswald, and Lieutenant Cox—were saved from having to choose sides thanks to President Washington's inadvertent aid, which took the form of a decree forbidding any American citizen to enlist or remain in the armies of the belligerents. The three officers immediately asked to be relieved of their military duties, and their request was granted.

The rumors making the rounds in Paris became even more alarmist after Dumouriez's defection. The Girondist government was losing its footing, its unpopularity increasing with the birth of the Revolutionary Tribunal during the cheerless spring of 1793. Camille Desmoulins, who had incited the mobs in the Palais Royal during the Revolution's brighter days, was now feeding the people's passions with his *History of the Brissotins*, an attack designed to whip up their anger against the deputies accused of complicity with Dumouriez. Desmoulins's ranting hastened the political demise of the Girondists—and eventually his own, for the demagogue's verbal excesses finally cost him his head. As Gouverneur Morris noted in a letter to the Countess of Albany: "The enormous wheel to which the fate of this empire is attached is crushing the very people who originally set it in motion. No one is strong enough to stop it, although everyone prides himself on thinking he can make it go where he chooses."

* The Duc d'Orléans, a cousin of the King, had, in a burst of revolutionary zeal, changed his name to Philippe Egalité.

The Revolution was at a crossroad. It had embarked on a crusade to rid the human race of its tyrants, but at the same time it had taught its missionaries how to speak up. Wasn't that why the Batavians, the Allobroges, and the people of Brabant had allowed themselves to disobey the King's injunctions? Now, free but disillusioned, they complained that they had simply replaced one master with another.

Gone were the days when the Revolution in full flower had awarded French citizenship to Europe and America and called on Thomas Paine to sit in the Convention. Little by little, all of England was being made to share in the sins of its king, and the inspired leadership of Dr. Richard Price and Joseph Priestley, the poems of Blake, and the appeals of James Mackintosh were soon forgotten.

This rampant nationalism made Americans uneasy, and it was rumored that even harsher xenophobic measures were in the offing, this time extending to France's allies as well. The Convention put its finger on the problem when it castigated "the perfidious means employed to call into question the intentions of its two faithful allies, the Swiss cantons and the United States." It reaffirmed its loyalty to its allies and expressed "its sentiments of candor, good will, and esteem."

But the Americans wanted proof, not words. A "delegation of North Americans established in France" submitted a petition to the deputies, congratulating them for the sentiments expressed in their kind decree. But, being practical men, they wanted to see these words translated into action and requested that a commission be appointed to examine the problem of commercial relations between France and "the vast family peopling the four corners of the world." Deputy Ramel pointed out that such a commission existed already, in the form of the Committee of Commerce. "I ask," he said, "that if the Committee of Public Safety so agrees, this committee be directed to make a prompt report on this important matter."

In the previous year, May and June had seen the beginning of the end of the Ancien Régime; the late spring of 1793 held a similar fate for the Girondists and the followers of Brissot. As the situation worsened and the weather brightened, expatriate Americans began to sigh for country retreats. After a series of negotiations with a former nobleman, one Turpin de Crissé, Gouverneur Morris bought his estate of Seine-Port, complete with furnishings, walled-in garden, outbuildings, and several acres of land. Ruth and Joel Barlow also thought it wise to spend the summer in the country and looked in the region of Meudon. Thomas Paine was so sickened by what was happening to the Revolution that he refused to set foot in the Convention, where he had been welcomed in triumph only eight months before. Determined to find himself a refuge until the return of better times, he rented rustic lodgings at 63 Faubourg Saint-Denis. His landlord, one Georget, had carved out several apartments in his farmhouse, their rent allowing him to lead a bucolic life devoted to his farmyard, vegetable garden, orchard, and fields. As neighbors, Paine had several Englishmen who were also seeking oblivion in the country and spent most of their time at outdoor sports. Paine took refuge in his work. *The Age of Reason* was taking shape—another appeal to common sense, this one exposing the Church. Occasionally he would put down his pen and pass the time of day with his neighbors or study the habits of his landlord's chickens, geese, and ducks.

Much against his will, Paine was forced to make a public

appearance during the month of May. Marat, to the loud applause of the *sans-culottes,* had accused the Convention of harboring a "cabal that had sold out to the British," and if the *Journal de Gorsas* is to be believed, he even advocated the massacre of several representatives.

Upon reading this appalling story in the papers, William Johnson, a slightly deranged young Englishman who was a neighbor and admirer of Thomas Paine, immediately assumed that his idol's life was threatened. Already unbalanced by the alarmist rumors circulating in Paris, the young man decided that he had had enough of human perversity and resolved to end his own life. He scribbled a few words of farewell to Paine and stabbed himself twice; the third stroke was stayed by a friendly hand, which also bandaged his wounds and restored the young man to life.

Brissot, hoping to turn this incident to political advantage, wrote in his newspaper, *Le Patriote français*:

> An Englishman, whose name I shall refrain from mentioning, renounced his country out of hatred for its kings; but all he sees in France is the mask of freedom hiding the hideous face of anarchy. Having decided to kill himself, he wrote these words presently in the possession of an illustrious foreigner: "I came to France to enjoy liberty, but Marat has destroyed it. . . . I can no longer bear the triumph of stupid inhumanity over talent and virtue."

The Brissotins and the Girondists still thought themselves strong enough to keep their opponents at bay. To muzzle Marat, they had him brought to trial. Among the many grievances they held against him, the "Johnson incident" was but a minor peccadillo. The public prosecutor, Fouquier-Tinville, was nonetheless determined to bring the affair into the open, and in due course, Brissot, Thomas Paine, William Johnson, and two other British subjects were summoned to appear before the court.

Questioned about the matter, Paine declared that young Johnson had been "suffering from mental anxiety" for some time, and that spleen, rather than Marat, was responsible for his act. Paine hardly knew Marat. As for Johnson's note, the one that had been quoted in *Le Patriote français*, Paine had showed it to Brissot without attaching the least importance to it. Nor did Johnson shed much light on the affair; when asked why he had tried to take his own life, he answered only, "My friendship for Thomas Paine pushed me to this extremity."

Popular feeling was running so strongly in Marat's favor that fear of mob violence forced the judges to back down, and the tribunal refrained from any form of condemnation.

Paine's solitude was interrupted again during the month of June. Fifty American ships had been interned in Bordeaux, and by order of the authorities, they had been immobilized for fear they intended to do business with England. The captains of the ships went to Paris to complain to Gouverneur Morris and ask that he intervene with the French to have their ships released. Morris agreed to help, but there was little enthusiasm in his protestations. Taking a purely legal tack, he coldly demanded a strict adherence to the agreements between the United States and France, which this embargo violated. Then he retired to Seine-Port.

Thrown back on their own devices and quite lost on the streets of Paris, the captains next turned to Thomas Paine. Paine alerted his friend Colonel Oswald, and the two men set off for Seine-Port to spur Morris into action. Morris greeted his visitors coolly. He did not care to have his name linked

185

with Paine, that "people's representative," even to extricate some Americans from a tight spot. When Paine reproached him for his lukewarm intervention and his reluctance to try again, the tone of their conversation sharpened. Finally Paine exploded: wasn't America's minister to France ashamed to be lining his pockets with the money of the government he served so ill? Vowing to see to the matter himself, and not to rest until his compatriots had gained satisfaction, Paine turned on his heels and left. Colonel Oswald, who had witnessed many an epic battle in his days with the Philadelphia press, took keen delight in the encounter: Gouverneur Morris was no friend of his.

Furious, Morris lost no time in writing to America: "Paine is agitating against me." It was probably quite true, for Paine had doubtless reported the details of his conversation with Morris to the American captains. In any event, during the next three months, he used what was left of his dwindling influence on behalf of the stranded sailors. In the end he advised them to draw up a petition and present it in person to the Convention, which they did on August 22. Admitted before the bar, they met with a sympathetic reception and managed to talk the deputies into allowing them to weigh anchor.

The Minister of Foreign Affairs pretended to be unaware of Paine's role in the affair when he informed Morris of the deputies' decision and added: "You should be highly pleased with the way in which the American captains were received." But this initial victory did not satisfy Paine. He wrote to Barère: "Approximately forty-five American vessels are now in Bordeaux. If the English want to take revenge on the Americans, these ships will be running serious risks during the crossing. The American captains left Paris yesterday, and I have urged them to ask the Convention to provide an escort for their ships."

As soon as the captains had left, Paine holed up in his lodgings and was heard from no more. The autumn was to be devoted to writing and meditating on *The Age of Reason*.

It was now the Girondists' turn to be thrown from the seat of power. Not content to see them outlawed, the fickle gods of the Revolution would end up asking for blood. The victorious Jacobin "Montagnards" tried to take up the reins and bring order out of confusion, but in vain. To civil disorder, unemployment, and famine were added the military disasters of June. Everything conspired against the government and favored its internal enemies—the royalists in hiding and the Girondists in retreat. How, under these conditions, could the Jacobins control the streets, reassure the wavering masses, and govern in an orderly manner?

Marat and the radical sheet *Père Duchesne* called on "Sainte Guillotine" as the only means capable of restoring order. The Committee of Public Safety at first turned a deaf ear to this outrageous proposition, but it had no other remedy to offer. Men of good will pondered how to check the spread of the disease. Similarly motivated, Charlotte Corday decided to help Providence. Unlike young Johnson whose hatred for Marat led him to offer himself as sacrifice, Charlotte Corday, resolving to set the world aright, bought a kitchen knife and killed Marat in his tub.

As so often happens when self-appointed arbiters take justice into their own hands, this naïve gesture only helped to open the floodgates; instead of stopping the infernal machine, it set the mob's passions on fire. After Marat's murder in July, the Girondists could not hope for leniency, and the aristocrats who had been lying low could no longer be overlooked. Thanks to Corday, the very heads that Marat and *Père Duchesne* had asked for, without success, would now roll.\* Meanwhile, with the loss of Mayenne and Valenciennes, Paris was again threatened with invasion. There was no choice for the leaders but to order a general conscription and all-out war. Fate was making tyrants of them, like it or not. Individual liberties disappeared with the passing of the Decree on Suspects in September; and with the *Maximum*, a law passed during the same month, economic liberty suffered the same fate.†

Edmond Charles Genêt's arrival in the United States threw more oil on the fire. After a rough crossing, he disembarked in Charleston, South Carolina, to a triumphal welcome. Three months of bad weather had so slowed communications between Europe and the United States that Americans were still unaware of the King's death and the declaration of war between France and Great Britain.

Before he had even contacted the American government or presented his credentials, Genêt was already spinning his web of intrigue in Charleston. The French consul, Michel-Ange Bernard de Mangourit, seconded Genêt's inflammatory projects, which fell on eager ears throughout the state. With Mangourit's help, Genêt came to an understanding with

---

\* The Reign of Terror that began in July was to last until the following summer. It was to claim the lives of members of all factions—Brissot and Vergniaud, Danton and Desmoulins, Robespierre and Saint-Just, and even Marie Antoinette fell victim to the guillotine.
† In August 1793, the draft became universal for all men between the ages of eighteen and twenty-five. A month later, the Convention enacted the first law of the *Maximum* as a method of keeping down the cost of living. Under these laws, the price of grain and other commodities was fixed.

General Moultrie, the governor of the state, who like most of his constituents was a fervent believer in the French Revolution.

Both North and South Carolina were delighted to see the French diplomats transform their states into a giant platform from which to launch military operations, fit out privateers, prey on British shipping, and raise troops to march on Florida and New Orleans—in short, to behave like masters in a conquered land. Likewise, Genêt proposed to influence public opinion by using the pro-French elements scattered about the country to weave a propaganda net across the United States.

After laying the preliminary groundwork in the South, the ambassador, booted and spurred, made his way north by road while the frigate that had brought him from France followed the coast to Philadelphia by sea. The ship made a detour to capture a British ship that thought itself safe in American waters. With its humiliated victim in tow, the *Embuscade* made a triumphal entry into the port of the American capital. A huge crowd was on hand to cheer the novelty of the spectacle. The ancient Romans had a habit of chaining their captives to their chariots, but this was a new and unexpected form of entertainment for the American public. This reception confirmed Genêt's faith in his lucky star, and he could only conclude that his mission was bound to succeed.

Unfortunately for Genêt, President Washington had just proclaimed America's neutrality. This should have warned Genêt that there were two sides to every coin, and that neither France nor indeed he himself could count on this sister republic as a friend. Alexander Hamilton had already used Louis XVI's execution as a pretext to declare that, with the death of the monarch who had signed the Franco-American alliance, the treaty was null and void. He had even suggested that the President should refuse to receive France's envoy.

In the opposing camp, Jefferson maintained that the treaty had been concluded not between the United States and Louis Capet, but between two nations, America and France, and therefore retained its legality. Kings pass, he remarked, but nations remain. President Washington accepted this point of view and granted Genêt an official audience as the minister of a friendly and allied nation.

The two men clashed at their very first meeting. Genêt started off by protesting that the declaration of neutrality violated the treaty of 1778. For his part, Washington remonstrated with the French diplomat for having taken improper initiatives and for showing disrespect for American sovereignty. Genêt inferred from this interview that "old Washington is jealous of my success and the enthusiasm with which the whole city is flocking to my door."

Hamilton despised him; Washington could not stand the sight of him; and now it was Jefferson's turn. Once so eager to extend his goodwill to the young minister fresh from revolutionary France, Jefferson was now disillusioned by Genêt's arrogance. The young upstart refused to listen to his counsel of moderation. Everything had to be done with a flourish; he despised restraints of any kind. Instead of quietly negotiating with Jefferson, he kept haranguing him, thrusting the 1778 treaty under Jefferson's nose with the demand that it be followed to the letter. He insisted not only that the United States should aid and abet France in its designs and let it use American ports as it pleased, but that it should also proceed with the payment of its debt to France so that the new republic could have the working capital necessary to fit out ships, raise troops, and finance its propaganda. Genêt closed on a menacing note: if the President and his Cabinet continued to put obstacles in his way, he would go right over their heads and appeal directly to the American people.

Jefferson was a man of reflection; how was he to reach an understanding with this provocateur who had no shred of respect for international law? He had trouble enough at cabinet meetings in the face of Washington's indifference and commitment to neutrality, not to mention Hamilton's intemperate advocacy of an alliance with England.

Meanwhile, passing from threats to action, Genêt had begun to incite insurrections, and the government had its hands full trying to contain the fire. At this point Jefferson became so disenchanted with Genêt that he rallied to Washington's views and accepted what he had originally called his "craven neutrality." Perhaps this makeshift solution would indeed prevent the worst, for the country was in no condition to embark on a war with Great Britain. But the solution went against the grain, and in the end, Jefferson refused to go along, offering instead to resign. Washington would not accept his resignation, and thus Jefferson had to remain at his post throughout 1793.

The Philadelphia Cabinet waited barely four months after Genêt's arrival before asking Paris for his recall. Unaware that the rug was being pulled out from under him, Genêt was full of assurance. Too far from France to gauge which way the wind was blowing, he continued to carry out the Girondists' directives, not only when the Girondists were fleeing for their lives but also when France was in the grip of the Terror.

That autumn, Genêt had finished recruiting the legions

that were to fight under the French flag against the Spanish territories on the borders of the United States. He gave the command of the first legion to General Clark, Thomas Paine's discovery, and the second to William Tate, a South Carolina officer. Tate's orders stated: "In the name of the French people, we, Genêt . . ." and continued with an invitation to "Citizen William Tate to recruit free and independent men desirous of serving under the flag of the republic in order to sever the chains of the oppressed and to form free companies of these virtuous enemies of tyranny and to organize them into a legion to be called the Revolutionary Legion of America." On October 15, Genêt made Tate a colonel on the strength of the powers granted him by the Girondist ministry and authorized the officer "to ask the consul in Charleston to give out any commissions that he might need for the officers under his orders."

From that time on, the legionnaires received their pay on a regular basis from the coffers of Genêt's organization. Some of this money came from the sale of booty taken from English ships captured by French privateers in flagrant violation of neutrality. Tate received a guinea a day, the superior officers a dollar, and lieutenants and ensigns a half-dollar. The officers were also given two dollars per head for each legionnaire recruited in the towns and three dollars for those brought in from the country. These new recruits were to be conveyed to a "general rendezvous" reminiscent of La Roüerie's Breton get-togethers.

Mangourit kept accounts and carefully meted out each *denier* to Tate. The consul was in his element; his only regret, as he told Genêt, was that the United States government was less indulgent toward French activities than were the compliant governments of the Carolinas. A good country,

Carolina: its citizens were not afraid of a few bumps and bruises, they believed in Franco-American friendship, and in Mangourit's words, appeared "to desire the invasion of Louisiana" with all their hearts.

Alarmed by the worsening situation, the American government finally resigned itself to arming forty ships and recruiting ten thousand men to protect its neutrality and defend its flag. Paris harbored the illusion that these measures were aimed at Great Britain alone, that America was on the verge of entering the war on France's side. When nothing of the sort happened, the French newspapers, unable to explain America's inaction, began to admonish its leaders from its side of the Atlantic. "Are you dead or paralyzed?" asked Duché in *Le Moniteur*. "Are not George III's orders to restrict your commerce a virtual declaration of war?" No. The American government viewed Britain's actions against its shipping not as a *casus belli* but as a threat to be warded off. Philadelphia was looking for something less extreme to loosen the British noose. Yet Duché insisted: "For you, France is Europe, and France alone should receive your exports. Paris and Philadelphia should be the two sides of the scales formed by our two hemispheres; your union with France will speed the fall of tyrants." After evoking the themes of brotherhood-in-arms and the blood shed in common for the cause of American freedom, he concluded with the admonishment that the United States be realistic and consider the material advantages of a rapprochement.

Certainly, George Washington had no love for English despotism, but he felt no attraction for the Terror either. Caught between the two evils, he chose the lesser and opted for negotiations.

The revolutionary press in France maintained a studied

silence concerning the acts of piracy committed by the French against American shipping while giving undue importance to the smallest sign of pro-French feeling in the United States. President Washington had only to murmur a criticism of the British for French papers to trumpet his every word, and when he declared to Congress that the United States would no longer tolerate the violation of its people's rights, the Paris gazettes presented this threat as being directed solely at British privateers. Little did they know that the American Cabinet was seriously thinking of sending a mission to lure the British into signing a pact of friendship with America.

In spite of his tense relationship with the government to which he was accredited, Genêt remained full of confidence. He had no way of knowing that during the autumn, the Paris press had begun to publish malicious stories about him. Early in the new year, *Le Moniteur* cracked its whip to denounce the liberty with which "a French republican had allowed himself to depart from the solemn principles of the Nation and to show disrespect for the rights of a people, its laws, and government. . . . Is it that our laws are so benumbed that they cannot punish such flagrant wrongdoing? Or must the people rise again and by their rigor make up for our lack of justice?" This allusion to Genêt's dealings served notice that the French press was going to use him as a scapegoat, accusing him of furthering British designs and acting as Pitt's right-hand man in America.

But the *sans-culottes* had no need to take to the streets demanding Genêt's recall, for the French government had already disavowed him and summoned him back to Paris to explain himself. He was made responsible for the worsening situation between the two countries at the very moment when the public was clamoring for closer bonds.

194

With Genêt's recall, that attractive post—far removed from the guillotine—became vacant. Citizen Deforgue, then Foreign Minister, immediately coveted the job, and to pave the way, he gave a few judicious dinners to which he invited Gouverneur Morris. However, Deforgue's aim fell wide of the mark, for the Committee of Public Safety appointed Joseph Fauchet to lance the abscess in Philadelphia.

No sooner had the United States expressed its grievances against Genêt than France responded with its own against Morris, and the recall of the one led to the recall of the other. Both men showed the same reluctance to leave their posts. Morris dug in his heels, stating that he must await the arrival of his successor in order to hand over the reins in person. As for Genêt, he lent a deaf ear to the injunctions from Paris, and abandoning both his diplomatic post and his machinations, went to make amends to President Washington and asked for political asylum in the United States, which was granted.

The task of restoring Franco-American friendship now fell to Joseph Fauchet. The French press, scarcely able to contain its enthusiasm, announced a few weeks after his nomination: "The entire American coast rejoiced at the sight of a French squadron of ten ships arriving at Hampton, Virginia, during the first days of February. There was even greater satisfaction in the knowledge that these vessels were bringing a new French minister to the United States."

To keep French spirits up, the Paris gazettes continued to report on Francophile reactions in America. One story involved a motion adopted by a Philadelphia town meeting at the suggestion of Stephen Girard, an American of French origin; another reported the existence of hitherto unknown Francophile communities in the United States, one being in Culpeper County, Virginia, on the Potomac River. Once

195

upon a time Frenchmen had marveled with Montesquieu that anybody could be a Persian, but since the Revolution they were beyond surprise, and it seemed perfectly normal that the inhabitants of Culpeper County should proclaim their affection for the French republic and offer to render it "any services compatible with its treaties." The citizens of Culpeper declared themselves to be the enemies of all kings and opposed to all rapprochements with the European monarchies, since no good could come of it. So much for the King of England and the supporters of the British alliance!

# 9

THE REVOLUTIONARY STORMS CAUSED MANY A SHIPWRECK, although the victims met with differing fates: some sank to the bottom; some, like Mme. Du Barry, managed to keep afloat for varying lengths of time; still others, like the Duchesse d'Anville and the Duchesse de La Rochefoucauld, bent with the wind and righted themselves in time.

Count Henry Seymour had broken off with Mme. Du Barry long before he left France and turned his Paris *hôtel* over to Gouverneur Morris. The Englishman, an eccentric like all his countrymen, assumed he had exclusive possession of Louis XV's former mistress while in fact she was giving the same attentions to the Duc de Brissac. Hence the British lord's anger and the subsequent rupture. From then on, the ripening lady continued to lead a sumptuous life at Louveciennes, spinning out her love affair with Brissac as the Ancien Régime unraveled.

In January 1791, Brissac gave a party at his *hôtel* on the rue de Grenelle and Mme. Du Barry stayed on for the night. She was awakened at dawn by her servants who had rushed to Paris from Louveciennes with the news that thieves had broken into the castle and stolen her jewels.

Mme. Du Barry immediately offered two thousand *louis* to anyone who could help track down the thieves, and had the announcement pasted on every wall in Paris. Curiously, no one seemed to take offense at this imprudent display of wealth. The jewels were traced to England, and the foolish woman set off in pursuit, escorted by Brissac's equerry, an expert jeweler, and several servants, among whom—without her knowledge—was an English spy.

For two years, she crossed and recrossed the Channel. The aristocracy in London treated her like exiled royalty, and Cosway painted her in full regalia, a necklace of pink pearls around her neck.

Even with the royal family imprisoned in the Temple, Du Barry continued her travels in a carriage driven by four horses. But warning signals were beginning to flash. One day, a band of revolutionaries penetrated her castle, seized a young officer hiding in a passage, and took him to prison where he met a tragic end. A few days later, they came back and threw the Duc de Brissac's freshly severed head over the garden wall. But none of this drama caused Mme. Du Barry to consider emigrating. She left for London in the autumn, not long after her last lover's massacre. The King's trial and execution took place during the five months she was away, and when the news of his death reached England, she went into boisterous mourning.

March found her back in Louveciennes. Her best silver and a few precious odds and ends having been hidden in fountains and under the manure pile, Du Barry wanted to get back to her nest and sit on her golden eggs.

As she crossed the threshold of the castle, she suddenly found herself face to face with a complete stranger, one George Grieve, a journalist and translator, born in England but claiming to be a United States citizen.

Grieve had lived in Paris during Franklin's tenure. He had often visited him in Passy, and it was Franklin who had had him swear allegiance to the United States before he agreed to give him a letter of recommendation to the New World. Franklin described him as "a warm and zealous partisan of America" who wished to settle there. But the United States was not able to keep its hold on George Grieve. He returned to France and settled in Marly, where he lived off the proceeds of minor literary efforts based on his knowledge of French and English. He made English translations of *Le Jeune Anacharsis*, Baron de Tott's impressions of the Turks and Tartars, *Voyages dans l'Amérique septentrionale* by Chastellux, as well as French versions of observations on the French Revolution by such illustrious authors as Dr. Richard Price and Joseph Priestley. His English origins never caused him trouble, for he was thought to be an American and a patriot in good standing.

Citizen Grieve had been keeping a sharp eye on Louveciennes, for he harbored a vengeful passion against Mme. Du Barry—a "bacchante crowned with ivy and roses," as he described her. When she left for London in pursuit of her jewels, he suggested that the theft was a ruse—"a beautiful excuse for emigrating."

He moved heaven and earth to see that the absent lady was put on the list of émigrés, but in vain. The "bacchante" kept slipping through his fingers, for she still enjoyed the state's favors. It was not until just before her final return to Louveciennes that he was able to have her house sealed and himself named as guardian.

When Mme. Du Barry arrived, he condescended to make room for the intruder, but continued to live in the castle while casting baleful looks in her direction. It did not take Du Barry long to realize that her days were numbered.

Grieve kept denouncing her to the Committee of General Security, but they exasperated him with their incompetence. Finally, the revolutionary authorities gave in, at least to the point of placing the suspect under surveillance in her own home, a far cry from Grieve's dream of prison and the scaffold.

Rising to the occasion, Mme. Du Barry wrote the local authorities: "Citizeness de Vaubernier Du Barry is astonished that with all the proof she furnished you for the reasons that compelled her to go to England, she is still being treated as an émigré."

Her insolence was too much for Grieve; he and a group of companions appeared at the bar of the Convention and demanded the sinner's head "in the name of morality." Once again, his hopes were dashed. Not only did the Convention do nothing, but the people of Louveciennes rose up in her defense, signing a petition in her name. Provoked beyond control, Grieve rushed to the Committee of General Security and forced them to issue a formal order for her arrest. Brandishing the paper, he requisitioned an armed detail and returned to Louveciennes to seize his prey and lead her to the prison of La Force. He knew that once she was caught in the Revolution's coils, nothing could save her. To close off all avenues of escape, Grieve assumed the role of devil's advocate. Free to roam the castle with its owner gone, he went over everything that threatened to bring a merciful verdict from the Revolutionary Tribunal. Leaving nothing to chance, he wrote his indictment, selecting those arguments most damning to the accused, and like a poisoned bouquet, presented it to the tribunal. In addition, he searched out witnesses with morbid delight, tracking them down, interrogating them, lecturing them, then classifying them according to the virulence of their feelings. The lukewarm were remorselessly cast aside.

He suffered a minor setback when one Citizen Jean Rat denounced him as "Grieve, American" and accused him of carrying on a secret correspondence with the traitor Dumouriez. But at long last, Du Barry's head did fall and Grieve was able to breathe again. That snake would hiss no more.

Logically, with Europe at war and France in the throes of revolution, the urge to travel should have diminished—not only for the unrepentant Du Barry but foreign tourists as well. Not at all. In 1793, as if the world were at peace, Colonel William Langborn was back in France from his extensive travels.

While Mme. Du Barry's comings and goings were conducted with the ceremony due a former king's mistress, Langborn went about casually, always on foot, living a frugal existence in whatever simple inn he happened upon. Last heard from in St. Petersburg, he had made his way back from the Near East, through Italy and the county of Nice, reaching France in the spring. His soul at peace, Langborn wandered through Provence, Languedoc, and Guyenne, finally ending up in Bordeaux. On arrival, he announced his intention to move on to Paris. The season was propitious and he expressed a wish to see the capital in its spring glory with the chestnut trees in bloom.

The United States consul, Joseph Fenwick, had already suffered the strange behavior of the terrible General Eustace. Now he was confronted with, to be sure, a much less offensive countryman, but one with equally extravagant plans.

"You intend to reach Paris on foot by way of the Vendée?"

"And why not?"

No word of the Chouans' uprising had reached the wanderer, always more alert to the song of birds than news of disaster. Fenwick raised his arms in disbelief, then described the peasants' rebellion with such eloquence that Langborn agreed to change his course and head for Spain.

Every kind of trouble awaited him on the far side of the Pyrenees. An American at large, coming from pestiferous France, in Spain for no valid reason, with an almost empty pocketbook, was bound sooner or later to find himself in prison. Lying on the straw in his Andalusian cell, Langborn cursed himself for having—this once—listened to the voice of wisdom. Had he followed his original impulse, he would have satisfied his curiosity about the Vendée and Paris with probably no damage to himself, and added zest to his travels in the bargain.

In December 1793, the Duchesse d'Anville and the Duchesse de La Rochefoucauld were caught in the net thrown by the Terror to catch suspect aristocrats. The two ladies were imprisoned in the Convent of the British Sisters on the rue des Fossés-Saint-Victor.

Meanwhile, William Short was in Madrid, where his government had sent him from The Hague to negotiate a treaty concerning the Florida and Mississippi boundaries. Already frantic to be done with his diplomatic chores and return to his beloved Rosalie, the rumor—still unconfirmed —that she and her grandmother had been arrested was more than he could bear. Lacking any news of their actual situation, he swallowed his pride and begged Gouverneur Morris to intercede with the government. Since he had no other intermediary, he sent his letters to Rosalie in care of Morris.

Communications between Spain and France being undependable at best, Short made several copies of each letter and sent them variously via England, the Low Countries, and Italy. One of these bottles cast into the sea had to reach its destination, and the act of repeating again and again the same expressions of anxiety somehow managed to soothe his anguish. At the same time, he ordered Van Staphorst, his Dutch banker, to dispatch money to France so that the duchesses would lack for nothing—their possessions having probably been confiscated.

Morris soon learned of the duchesses' whereabouts and set off on the Boulevard Saint-Germain, now empty of carriages. The Convent of the British Sisters was situated at the bottom of a hill just below the Panthéon, looking out over the King's gardens, the Seine, and the Ile Saint-Louis, while its mournful entrance faced the muddy, sunless confines of the Fossés-Saint-Victor. A flight of stairs connected the street to a small paved courtyard where the concierge held sway. A little farther was the parlor, and next to it the cloisters whose arches framed pots of winter-killed plants. Inside the cloisters was a small square of lawn with a well in the center. Visitors were forbidden to go beyond the cloisters or into the handsome gardens that faced the city. A low wall separated the convent from its neighbors, the Convent of the Sisters of Mercy and the Scottish College; on the far side lay open country.

Revolutionary prisons were set up wherever space could be found, and some were quite surprising: the Convent of the British Sisters had kept the look of a well-maintained boarding school; prodded by their mother superior, "Mrs." Canning, the sisters were mindful of its appearance.

In their tidy apartments, the two duchesses looked as if they were making a retreat. Their faithful servants, Mme.

Postulard and Mlle. Raffron, had asked to go with them to prison. Educated women of good breeding, they passed the time reading to the ladies. Mme. Postulard's husband and the other servants who had remained either at the Hôtel de La Rochefoucauld in Paris or at the Château de La Roche-Guyon provided daily deliveries of food and other necessities. The heavier work was done by women from the neighborhood, and another prisoner, Citizeness Blanchet, an expert laundress, was put in charge of their linen.

Blanchet had been a servant of Abbé de Salamon, the Papal representative in Paris; when he fled, she was imprisoned in his place. Because of her soft hands, the Duchesse d'Anville chose her to dress the wounds on her legs from which she had long suffered. The Revolution had freed people's tongues—including even those of priests' servants—and since Blanchet had heard the name La Rochefoucauld associated with several of the Devil's disciples, such as Voltaire, Condorcet, and Lafayette, she used her ministrations to the duchess's legs as occasions to make bold observations on the subject of aristocrats who had sown the wind and reaped the whirlwind.

When the young duchess welcomed Gouverneur Morris into the convent parlor, she tried to make her greeting warmer than the one she had given him the year before at court. However much she might welcome the letter in his hand, it must have crossed her mind that had Morris not usurped Short's place and chased him from Paris, her own true love might be the man standing in front of her now. Be that as it may, she thanked him for the letter and Morris took away her own.

In March 1794, still unsure of the duchesses' whereabouts, Short wrote Rosalie: "After a very long interval I received from Mr. Morris . . . his two letters of the 16th October and the first of January. They brought me at the same time your dear letters of the 10th of October and the 30th of December. It was the first intimation I had had that you were no longer at La Roche. . . ." In July, he wrote:

> It is a long time, my dearly beloved friend, since I have received news of you . . . but I am so accustomed to misfortune and the future looms so dark that I hardly dare hope for anything. . . . How I decry the cruel fate that took me so far from you! What a difference there would have been in our lot had I remained in France working for my country in the capacity in which I was. Today would have found us united, we should never have had to be parted. . . . If you insist on remaining with your grandmother—and I admit that her age and your devotion to her would demand it—I shall never again leave you but shall ask permission of my government to remain in Paris.

And he ended with the *cri de coeur:* "Farewell, my dearest and most cherished friend, let us cling to the hope that heaven, which has united us, will put an end to our long and cruel separation. That is the only hope I have. I am confident, as I have always been, that our vows were not made in vain."

If William Short's misfortunes were of the heart, the English in Paris were the prey of the Revolutionary government. William Johnson was still living with Thomas Paine on the Faubourg Saint-Denis when he learned of the decree calling for the imprisonment of all British subjects. He managed to escape to Switzerland with a friend.

Helen Maria Williams was less fortunate: she, her mother, and her sisters were forced to endure the rigors of the Palais du Luxembourg for several weeks. As soon as she was granted her freedom, she fled to Basel. And thanks to Gilbert Imlay,

Mary Wollstonecraft was able to obtain a passport through Gouverneur Morris' kind offices that bore the name "Mrs. Imlay, American." The constraints of the times encouraged fraud, and counterfeit papers of identity blossomed along with counterfeit money. All kinds of measures were aimed against foreigners. Only the Americans remained untouched, and during one discussion at the Convention, Bazire even proposed to exclude from the law's reach all wives of United States citizens, regardless of their place of birth, including subjects of George III.

This placed Thomas Paine, an American and an elected delegate to the Assembly, in an ambiguous position. During Louis XVI's trial, some gazettes pretended not to know his true nationality: "The Englishman, Thomas Paine, is acting dishonorably in sharing Brissot's opinions."

With the Girondists eliminated and the deputy from the Pas-de-Calais in his self-imposed exile in the suburbs, Barère took the convention floor to challenge a foreigner's right to represent the French people. Bourdon de l'Oise went a step farther and declared: "Thomas Paine's patriotism has been praised. Well, ever since Brissot's henchmen disappeared from the Convention, he has not set foot inside the Assembly, and I also happen to know that he is in league with a former agent of the Foreign Office."

Thuriot spoke up next, accusing Paine of having consistently voted "with known traitors to their country." Bentabolle capped the accusations with the demand that "during the war, all foreigners be excluded from excercising public functions," to which the Convention lent a favorable ear.

Where were the days when the Revolution embraced all brothers from every corner of the universe? The wheel had turned and Paine felt the growing threat.

For other Americans, the only risk lay in being confused with the English. And in times like those, little was needed to raise the suspicions of impassioned patriots.

Such was the experience of a Baltimore merchant named Thomas Waters Griffith. On his return from a trip to England, he was so intimidated by the National Security Police that he appeared embarrassed when answering their questions. This, together with his hesitant French and lack of address, damned him, and he was led straight to prison where he spent two months. William Haskins of Boston was jailed as a British spy. But since both men enjoyed good reputations in Paris business circles, their friends managed to get them out and they resumed their activities none the worse for wear.

Major William Jackson's incarceration lasted little more than a day. Born in England, like Paine, he too had become a fervent republican and won his spurs with the American rebels. In 1781 he accompanied Colonel John Laurens to Versailles, where the United States Congress had directed them to seek a new loan. The mission was successful, and Colonel Laurens left for America with two and a half million silver francs bulging in his bags. But Jackson decided to stay on. When he returned home at last, it was to become George Washington's collaborator—first in a military capacity, then, in 1789, as a civilian. Torn between service to his country and his commercial interests, he interrupted his official duties to make another trip to Europe in 1789.

Ten years after his first trip to France, Major Jackson gave up his post with Washington and threw in his lot with an influential businessman named William Bingham. Now he was in Europe to sell land owned by Bingham in the region of the Saint Lawrence River.

Jackson had gone first to London to prepare for his trip to Paris. It was November 1793, at the very time that Marie Antoinette—whose hand he had kissed at Versailles—was climbing the steps to the scaffold. In December, Jackson disembarked at Boulogne, together with three other Americans. When their baggage was being examined, some suspicious papers turned up in one of their cases. That was all the local authorities needed to assume that they were all Englishmen disguised as Americans. They were arrested forthwith "as a precautionary measure," and their case was submitted to Paris.

Gouverneur Morris took little interest in their misfortune and did nothing to help. Luckily for the detainees, the Committee of Public Safety looked over the dossiers sent from Boulogne, declared the men to be "irreproachable patriots," and ordered their release. To repay them for their poor welcome, and "anxious to offer our American brothers proof of union and fraternity," the committee granted Jackson and his traveling companions authorization to move freely throughout the republic.

Their only desire was to reach Paris, where Major Jackson made straight for his country's representative and berated him for his inaction. The blow-up between the two men was soon known to everyone in the American colony, and all those hostile to Morris took Jackson's side. Soon after, it was the major's turn to be importuned on a countryman's behalf: Thomas Paine had just been arrested.

With his house forcibly emptied of its British tenants, Paine had gone into melancholy retirement and dedicated himself to his work. The last pages of *The Age of Reason* were finished in December, just in time to allow Paine to celebrate the end of the year with his friend Achille Audibert. Not daring to be separated from his manuscript, Paine took it with him to Audibert's lodgings in the Maison de Philadelphie in the passage des Petits-Pères.

During this period, Paris was often aroused from its sleep by the noise of house arrests and the accompanying sounds of horses' hooves, running feet, pounding on doors, barked commands, and the clang of weapons. The night of December 27, 1793, was passing quietly enough when Citizen Doilé, the police commissioner, appeared at the Maison de Philadelphie with his secretary and a military escort. He woke the porter and thrust under his nose a warrant for the arrest of one of the tenants, whom he was to escort to prison in the Palais du Luxembourg.

Revolutionary justice was implemented by a punctilious bureaucracy, and its demands were expressed in torrents of documents decorated with Roman fasces, Phrygian helmets, heraldic devices, seals, and elaborate signatures.

The porter examined the paper, and, finally deciphering Thomas Paine's name, led the police to the old pamphleteer's room. To confirm the identity of the citizen blinking at him from his bed, Commissioner Doilé asked: "Thomas Paine?"

"Thomas Paine."

His identity established, the dialogue ended there. As the commissioner wrote in his meticulous report: "We couldn't make ourselves understood as he was American."

Audibert emerged from a neighboring room to serve as interpreter. Having inspected Paine's meager baggage and learned that he was only a temporary guest, the police asked where he lived and where he kept his papers. Commissioner Doilé announced that he would take Paine to the given address so that they could conduct the search in his presence.

209

Day was breaking as Paine dressed himself. Audibert and the porter got into a conversation with the police and commiserated with them for having to get up before dawn to perform such exhausting duties and with so much zeal. At this demonstration of compassion, the police sighed deeply. The fact was that they were perishing from hunger. Nothing to it: a meal could be put together in no time. Always the scrupulous civil servant, Doilé included the invitation in his report: "Finding ourselves in a state of exhaustion, we were forced to take nourishment."

Only a year earlier, to the joyous clatter of dishes, the Anglo-Americans in Paris had celebrated the victories of Valmy and Jemmapes in this very place, with toast after toast downed to the love of mankind and liberty.

In spite of the hard times, the cellar and kitchen of the Maison de Philadelphie were not without provisions. The diners remained at table until eleven o'clock in the morning, which gave Paine and Audibert time to work out their plan of operation. Indifferent to his own fate, Paine cared only for his manuscript. It must be hidden somewhere, and if entrusted to Joel Barlow, it was assured of publication.

As good humor emanated from their wine glasses, the police lent a kindlier ear to Paine's suggestion—as interpreted by Audibert—and Commissioner Doilé agreed to convey the prisoner to the home of his fellow countryman and friend, Joel Barlow. The commissioner did not report whether a little corruption buttered the transaction.

When the prisoner and his protective guard made ready to leave, Commissioner Doilé invited Paine into his waiting carriage and ordered the coachman to head for the rue Jacob where the Barlows lived in what was then known as the Maison de Bretagne. Paine and Barlow exchanged a few words, Barlow took possession of the precious manuscript, then he in turn was permitted to take a seat in the carriage. En route to the prisoner's house, Doilé stopped the carriage at the Committee of General Security so as to take on an official interpreter. Citizen Etienne-Thomas Dessous was available and joined them in the carriage. Doilé noted in his report that "Citizen Barlow would thus work together with Citizen Etienne-Thomas Dessous in the examination of the English texts." So the loaded carriage rattled across Paris to the northern suburb under the watchful eye of the police.

Paper being Thomas Paine's principal nutrient, his house contained little else. Notes and jottings overflowed his work table, spilling onto chairs and the floor where correspondence lay scattered among gazettes, books, Convention reports, and brochures, not to mention the papers that filled his drawers.

Undismayed by the disorder, the commissioner pushed the printed matter to one side and concentrated on the manuscripts, separating those written in English from those in French. For the sake of convenience, the examination of the manuscripts was transferred to the drawing room. A true professional, the commissioner noted in his report that the room was lit "by three windows, one looking over the garden, the others over the courtyard."

Paine's spirit was at rest, for his masterpiece was far from the commissioner's prying eyes, in Barlow's safekeeping. Its custodian would protect it well, and with Lanthenas and de Bonneville to help, its publication in French was assured.

Doilé dictated the report to his secretary, the brief glance at the prisoner's papers having metamorphosed into "the most scrupulous examination." He signed it, and Paine, Barlow, and Dessous placed their signatures at the bottom of the page as witnesses. By then it was four in the afternoon and getting dark.

Everybody got back into the carriage, Paine with a few

odds and ends rolled into a bundle, and the outing resumed, this time in a southerly direction. Once they had passed the Collège des Quatre-Nations, Barlow asked to be dropped off; by the time the rest of the group reached the Luxembourg prison, it was pitch dark.

To effect the transfer of his prisoner, Doilé had to prove the legality of the arrest. Benoît, the head guard, took out his register and proceeded with the formalities of committal. The interpreters having disappeared, Paine complied silently with the guard's motions and signed where indicated. A prison warden then took his new charge in hand and led him toward his destiny with professional detachment.

A true Bourbon, Monsieur, the King's brother, had abandoned the Palais du Luxembourg, preferring Versailles to Paris. Seven years earlier, John Trumbull, the painter, had asked to look at the Rubenses in the palace gallery, and permission had been granted—with great reluctance, for the apartments were in ruins, and even with supporting trusses, the ceilings threatened to fall down on visitors' heads.

When the court left Versailles after the October Days, Monsieur resigned himself to moving into the Petit-Luxembourg, but he quietly passed beyond the frontiers at the very same time that the royal family was being arrested at Varennes. Being cleverer than his brother, Monsieur knew how to avoid ambushes.

The Palais du Luxembourg retained its princely attributes thanks to its proud architectural lines, noble proportions, and impressive entrances. The lighting, however, left something to be desired. Weak lanterns and smoking candle stubs had replaced the crystal and silver chandeliers. As Thomas Paine crossed the antechambers and drawing rooms overlaid with gilt, the dim democratic lighting obscured the decorated ceilings and filthy floors, and his phantom reflection was caught only here and there in the few mirrors that remained.

While Achille Audibert was preparing a plea for the prisoner, Joel Barlow was gathering together a group of Americans to make a formal appeal before the Convention. They presented themselves at the bar with a request for the prisoner's release, leaving a detailed petition in the hands of the president. Starting early in January 1794, Barlow collected eighteen signatures and won the support of Major Jackson, the newest arrival, who agreed to head the delegation.

Thomas Paine had been vegetating in prison for a month when the American delegation appeared before the bar. Behind Jackson stood Joel Barlow, Samuel Blackden, Mark Leavenworth, and eleven other Americans. The spokesman pleaded for that "apostle of American liberty, esteemed philosopher, and virtuous citizen" whom the French nation had once granted the honor of representing it, only to throw him in jail where he had been languishing a month. The Republic had no case against him; the examination of his papers had revealed only "his love of liberty" and confirmed "the principles of public morality that won him the hatred of kings and the love of his fellow citizens."

"Citizen representatives, we ask you in the name of liberty's friends, in the name of your allies, the American people, your brothers, do not give the coalition of despots— and above all the British tyrant (who committed the dastardly act of banishing him)—the pleasure of seeing Paine in chains!"

And Jackson concluded with the proposition: "Legislators, if you will permit us to return Thomas Paine to his brothers in America, we will answer for his conduct during the time he is to remain in France."

Vadier, who was presiding, answered with equal fervor:

"Stalwart Americans, our friends in liberty, and animated by a mortal hatred of all tyrants," he began, going on to extol the friendship of the two sister republics. But, as he had his feet firmly on the ground, he took the occasion to examine the practical aspects of the nations' relationship: "If the tree of liberty is to blossom in the two hemispheres, commerce must also—through this happy alliance—cast the shade of its burgeoning branches over the two poles." And how to bring this about? Well, all that was necessary was for the United States to join France in order "to crush, in concert, those arrogant islanders, those insolent would-be masters who desire to dominate the seas and nations' commerce."

And where was poor old Paine in all this?

Vadier reined in his eloquence just long enough to cast a thought in his direction: "Citizens, you ask us to release Thomas Paine; you want to take this defender of the rights of man home. We can but applaud your generous action."

There was a little desultory applause. Clearly, the Convention was unmoved. What of Danton, Hérault de Séchelles, Abbé Sieyès, and Abbé Grégoire? Where was the affection they had always shown the prisoner?

After his eulogy, Vadier's tone took on a certain reserve. If the prisoner—that true apostle of liberty—had given such powerful aid to the American Revolution, "his genius" had remained indifferent "to the one coming into being in France." It was clear that in this unfortunate situation, Paine's countrymen could expect little more than delaying tactics. "The National Convention will take your petition under advisement and will invite you to its session."

Paine's case was turned over to the Committee of Public Safety and its agent, the Committee of General Security. This was the death blow to the Americans' efforts. Their own representative had refused to give his aid. A protest from Morris, in his capacity as United States minister, might have intimidated the French government. Gouverneur Morris remained silent. Later, after Robespierre's execution in July of 1794, this surprising statement turned up in the dead man's intimate journal: "Ask that Thomas Paine be arraigned, for America's sake as well as that of France." Who could have made Robespierre invoke "America's sake" if it were not the United States representative himself?

The author of *Common Sense* was not always the best practitioner of the qualities he extolled: his illusions about Gouverneur Morris prevented him from recognizing the depths of the minister's baseness. As United States minister, Morris was the only person the prisoner was allowed to communicate with beyond the confines of the Luxembourg. Paine kept entreating him to protect his rights as an American citizen, but in vain. Eventually, however, his countrymen's petition did force Morris to make certain moves lest he one day be accused of inaction. Always looking to the future and its imponderables, Morris wrote Citizen Deforgue, the Foreign Minister, that Paine—born British, only lately become an American, and subsequently French—was not really his responsibility. He did ask the minister for an answer to his letter, because he needed to have some vindicating piece of paper in hand, something that would give the impression—should he ever need it—that he had indeed intervened for the prisoner.

"Please, if there are any reasons opposing his release, let me know what they are."

The British Cabinet maintained an informer in Paris named Monro who, taking great pleasure in Paine's misfortunes, sent the Foreign Office a report noting that Thomas

Paine was moving heaven and earth to be recognized as an American citizen, but that the United States minister was far too clever to let such a fish swim freely in his waters, and he had therefore told Robespierre that he had no knowledge of any rights of naturalization that Paine could lay claim to.

In an official dispatch to his government, Morris wrote that, contrary to information in British newspapers, Paine had not been guillotined, for the Montagnards held him in too much contempt to let him share the same fate as the Brissotins. The dispatch included the detail that Paine "amuses himself with publishing a pamphlet against Jesus Christ."

Here, Morris was wrong: Paine was plotting no such attack. He considered Christ a victim whose corpse had been exploited by his executioners' descendants since the earliest days of Christianity. On the other hand, he did attack the various Christian sects, and just as he had accused the Pope of using his imperialist policies to shine Caesar's boots and run the world, he castigated the Reformation for substituting the infallibility of the Bible for that of the Pope.

Even as he put the last words to *The Age of Reason*, Paine knew that he had far from exhausted his subject. Ideas still spun about in his head. He came to see that *The Age of Reason* needed a second part in which he could denounce the nursery tales, travesties, contradictions, and immorality of the sacred book. Being imprisoned, he gave himself completely to his work. If anyone mentioned his exclusion from the Convention, he simply shrugged.

In that vast palace filled to every insalubrious corner, the prisoners made the best of things. Many of the aristocrats had brought their own servants; their less fortunate neighbors depended on Benoît, the concierge, and his wardens. For a small consideration, they cleaned the rooms, took care of the fire, trimmed the candles, and laid the table for the meals sent in by caterers. They also did the laundry, brought in newspapers, and delivered more or less clandestine letters. The prisoners visited and dined together, played cards, and gossiped into the small hours. Around the Duchesse d'Orléans, court protocol was strictly observed as far as possible, even as death hovered over those who came to bow before the great lady. The Luxembourg registry also included several British officials captured at Toulon; Louis-Guillaume Otto, Lyonnet's former correspondent in the Foreign Office; Citizen Deforgue, the recent Foreign Affairs minister and rejected candidate to succeed Genêt in Philadelphia; and Danton, whose arrival at the Luxembourg with his followers caused a ripple of laughter among the prisoners.

Prison life grew more difficult with the coming of spring. Deciding that the inmates were much too comfortable, the Inspector of Prisons tightened discipline, replaced the kindly Benoît, forbade visits and newspapers, and packed off the servants who had accompanied their masters.

Letters still penetrated the walls, and one day Paine received a mysterious communication from an unknown lady. Signed "A little corner of the world," the note was purportedly written to dissipate his melancholy. His correspondent was the wife of a British banker in Paris, Sir Robert Smyth, who had been one of the guests at the Hôtel White banquet celebrating the victories at Valmy and Jemmapes. A short while before Paine's arrest, Smyth's wife had gone to see Paine in his suburban retreat to ask him to intervene for a man under suspicion. She did not know that he no longer attended the Convention, nor that he had lost all influence. But their conversation must have uncovered subjects of mutual concern, since the good lady had indulged in this innocent mystification to bring him a breath of the outside world. Cheered by this unexpected letter, the old Don Quixote answered in the same vein, signing his effort, "A castle in the clouds."

But Paine's health began to deteriorate, and doctors became his daily companions, first Dr. Makouski, the prisoners' official doctor, then two British physicians who were also prisoners, Dr. Bond and Dr. Graham.

For the majority of the Convention in 1793, liberty in economic affairs had begun to take precedence over all other forms. The republican assembly was infected by Turgot's liberal principles as had been the Constituent Assembly before it. The Convention reckoned that sound administration meant "laissez-faire" as well as "laissez-passer." Still, the zealots shouted for a tax on cereals to limit the merchants' profits. The liberals, even the boldest and most radical among them, like Robespierre, thought this utopian; to them, the law of the *Maximum* was a demagogic apple offered up to popular greed.

All the same, this dangerous fruit ripened with the warm weather. When autumn came, it fell of itself, and the majority saw that they had to accept the *Maximum* as the only effective remedy for the republic's ailments; once the economy had been put to rights, they would do what they could to juggle private interests for the benefit of the masses. If the tax on grain was not enough to control the cost of living, taxation would be extended to include meat, fish, wine, sugar, coal, fats, oil—including candles and soap—as well as paper, metals, cloth, and tobacco.

The Americans in Paris were importing a large number of these products, and they did not care for the projected measures. But they could do little about them. They knew only too well the difficulties France was going through, and they accepted the new rulings even if these went against their own interests. Perhaps ways could be found to make accommodations with the law, or to get around the restrictions with a little help from certain representatives—the committees where they had secret intelligence or civil servants in the various offices. Come what may, they would remain the nation's providers.

Braving all dangers, international smuggling went into high gear. Along the Atlantic coast and as far as the Baltic Sea, neutral merchants took up strategic posts from which to spy on the belligerents, ready to furnish their needs. Ships flying the American flag continued to sail the seas, even doing business—more or less clandestinely—with the warring countries. And from Britain they imported into France the products the republic's army needed to wage war against Britain.

Several Americans had a foot on both sides of the Channel, shamelessly forging links between Paris and London. Why else would Mark Leavenworth, Daniel Parker, and Benjamin Hitchborne have gone into partnership to charter the *Cumberland*? Its papers in order, the schooner left its British port with a cargo of rice and flour destined for Bilbao in Spain. As it reached the mouth of the Gironde under full sail, it suddenly tacked toward Bordeaux, where everything was in readiness to receive its cargo.

Gilbert Imlay was not the only one to make subterfuge the handmaiden of trade, but he was able to maintain such secrecy that his machinations left hardly a trace. Only Colonel Blackden was beset with failure upon failure, to the point that he finally gave up and returned with his wife to the United States.

219

Joel Barlow was another of the speculators, but thanks to his astuteness and good connections in high places, he was an invaluable aid to his partners. When, at the end of 1793, Robespierre organized a purchasing commission, Barlow made immediate contact with its three members and thus obtained the import permits that were indispensable to his associates' operations.

The captains of the American ships anchored in French ports tendered potassium, tobacco, and whale oil as well as sugar and indigo. In one single catch, the Committee of Supplies acquired the entire cargoes of a dozen American ships in the port of Le Havre. The committee paid out over six million francs, although it refused three thousand pairs of shoes as being of poor quality and "exorbitant price." In return, the merchant-captains asked permission to take on certain luxury items permitted under the *Maximum*. The Committee of Public Safety consented, on condition they were paid in silver and not paper money.

The Committee of Supplies shuttled between exporting cognac, salt, lace, and silk stockings and importing sometimes quite unknowable items. One day it was dickering with Joel Barlow to lower his price on potassium; the next day it was bargaining with Benjamin Jarvis for the purchase of 225 sheets of tin plate scattered among a thousand crates. Or it was asking Jesse Putnam and Benjamin Callender to clarify the "several objects of prime necessity" that the two traders were offering without specifying their nature. Then it made a deal to buy straw from John Rush and John Orr while refusing the tobacco offered by John Ewing, an agent for the house of Cunningham and Company in Philadelphia. When Citizen Rotch, the Nantucket whaler, offered his reserves of whale oil stored in Dunkirk and Amiens, the committee quietly invited the officials of the two cities to requisition the oil.

The Americans were not always safe from the vagaries of the French, and the impetuous ways of the French sailors gave them considerable trouble as well. On one occasion, the American ship *The Little Cherub*, which was owned by Thomas Ramsden, a merchant highly esteemed in Paris circles, put into port at Le Havre, where it left off fifty Frenchmen it had taken on board to protect them from Spanish brutality. The ship's captain went through the proper formalities and set sail for Hamburg. Once in the Channel, the ship was set upon by the French lugger *Argus* and the privateer *Le Vrai Patriote* (with little regard for its name). As its assailants went through the ship, the captain and his crew offered no resistance. A useless show of docility. One of the pirates suddenly leapt on a second lieutenant, took him by the throat, then let him go only to shoot him dead.

Ramsden protested to the Convention, and basing his plea on a recent decree, requested the court at Dunkirk to furnish him with all information relative to the affair. He assembled his dossier and submitted it to the Convention, demanding damages with interest. Barère, who had been charged by the Committee of Public Safety to handle the matter, concurred in the plaintiff's conclusions; the Assembly agreed, Ramsden was vindicated, and *The Little Cherub*'s aggressors were denounced.

This did not, however, discourage further acts of piracy. Henry Preble became a victim when one of his ships carrying tobacco to London was seized by the inhabitants of a coastal village and taken to Boulogne, its sails torn and ropes cut. There were so many incidents, followed by so many recriminations, that by the end of 1793 a decree was passed to control the war on cargo ships. But the new decree was flouted to the point where within two months, the inhabitants of Brest had the pleasure of watching several captured American vessels triumphantly led into port.

These captures and the lawsuits that resulted were disquieting to merchants in Paris, naturally concerned for their profits, and the comings and goings of their ships sailing the Atlantic and the Channel gave them many an anxious moment.

General John Skey Eustace's name did not figure among those who signed the petition for Thomas Paine, even though their shared love of liberty and hatred of kings should have made them friends. Perhaps he was never asked to sign, living as he did on the fringes of the American circle in Paris, which he held in contempt.

Eustace lived a Spartan existence, locked up with his books, far from Paris pleasures and café gossip. He seemed to admire only two men in Paris: the Dutch banker Jacob Van Staphorst, who had been exiled by the Orangemen for his liberal opinions, and one Professor Denis, a scholar and atheist who helped Eustace with his study of ancient and modern languages. Once the lesson was over, student and teacher turned to politics. Eustace vented his ire against his numerous *bêtes noires,* the King of England being his favorite target, and Denis lent him a sympathetic ear.

Unfortunately for Eustace, the dialogue came to a sudden end, for Denis took it into his head to marry. If the teacher was so foolish as to prefer conjugal intimacy to his student's observations, the general had no intention of abandoning the weapons he had so carefully honed during their many tête-à-têtes. Thereafter he devoted his solitude to expressing his indignation in the form of vitriolic letters to his faithless friend. Adopting a familiar style—"as if I were talking to you"—he listed George III's abominations and particularly his insolence at naming the little orphan in the Temple "King of France" and "Louis XVII." Moreover, after the seizure of Toulon, the shameless sovereign had stated that the British fleet's success was but a first step toward the restoration of the Bourbons with this child as king. To this, Eustace exploded: "A bastard governing twenty-five million Frenchmen!"

Epigrams and quotations garnished his correspondence like so many truffles; he cited Marmontel, Abbé Raynal, Rousseau, Swift, Robespierre, Franklin, not to mention Montesquieu and Cervantes. In passing, he made mention of his own military prowess, castigated Miranda, and ridiculed his countrymen in France. To him, they were suspect veterans of the War of Independence and overbearing heroes who paraded their military rank instead of imitating his example by volunteering in the armies of the French Revolution. These officers had isolated themselves within their self-indulgent prosperity, heedless to the need to defend liberty against the tyrants' threats.

Citizen Denis was too preoccupied with his honeymoon to translate Eustace's text into French. Eustace had to resort to a printer who published the brochure in English as "Letters on the Crimes of George III, Addressed to Citizen Denis by an American Officer in the Service of France." Eustace personally distributed his pamphlet to a few people who knew English, particularly members of the Convention, while other copies found their way to England. Having shot off his arrow, the former member of Dumouriez's staff left France to try Switzerland's brand of liberty.

# 10

WHILE THOMAS PAINE WAS INCARCERATED IN LUXEMBOURG prison, the fluctuations in the value of money and securities were tempting wilier men to juggle *assignats,* gold *louis,* and *écus,* and to exploit the Revolution as profiteers.

To assure the victory of the French armies and provide the people with their daily bread, the Convention dealt with merchants and financiers through its Committee of Supplies. Merchants eager for orders haunted the various services, plotted with the committees and ministries, and corrupted with the best of them. The Americans exchanged their cargoes for any species offered—metal or paper, letters of credit, *assignats,* merchandise for export, or even art objects purloined from the Crown's estates. They fattened their hoard, but not without running serious risks.

Since the coming of winter boded ill and shortages threatened the civilian population as well as the armies, the Convention decided to send a convoy to the United States in quest of food and ammunition. Comprising six regular cargo ships and five frigates, the convoy also carried a purchasing commission made up of trustworthy citizens who had been given the sum of 1.4 million francs sterling to pay for their purchases.

When he heard this news, Michael O'Mealy, a Baltimore man who lived in a furnished room at the Hôtel Thomas du Louvre, addressed a report to the Convention explaining that it was most unwise to send Frenchmen to the United States as buyers. At the mere announcement of their coming, prices would skyrocket; the American merchants, well informed about France's needs and equally able to surmise the degree of the foreigners' ignorance, would have the upper hand and fleece them. O'Mealy spoke plainly: "Citizens, stop what you are doing and call back your buyers. In their stead, send an honest, energetic agent who knows these people but whose purposes would not be known to them." And, he continued, secrecy was essential if they were to get a good price; an American citizen, wandering innocently between New York, Philadelphia, Baltimore, and Alexandria, with a single ship rather than a conspicuous armada, would arouse no one's suspicions and outwit unscrupulous speculators. The O'Mealy method detailed how the clever buyer should begin with evasive tactics, in this case throwing sand in the seller's eyes by telling him that northern European countries were already providing supplies to the French navy; immediately, American hopes would be dashed, and as a result there would be a saving of 25 to 30 percent on the final bill of sale. "By following this procedure, you thwart these swindlers' dastardly projects and prevent their growing rich at the expense of your liberty and happiness."

Citizen O'Mealy then proposed his own candidacy: "As an inhabitant of a free country, I would be honored to serve the French republic. Should I be so lucky as to be selected by her, I will serve her loyally. And I should like to point out to the Committee that with my knowledge of America, I am in a position to be more useful there than in any other country."

This curious statement had its own peculiar logic. Mindful

of his Irish origins, O'Mealy was ready with an alternative: if the Republic decided not to send him across the Atlantic, he would offer to go to Ireland, where soap and candles, raw and tanned hides, and cloth were cheaper than anywhere else. Specifically, he would propose to order shirts for the army's soldiers at prices below all other competitors.

Meanwhile, Joseph Fenwick, United States consul in Bordeaux but also a partner in the American firm of Fenwick, Mason and Company, was thinking about the commercial relationship between the two countries. He communicated the results of his reflections to the Committee of Supplies. He told them that his countrymen found the relationship between their two countries too uncertain and wished to see it regularized. The recent partial and precarious measures taken by France were detrimental to American business ventures, the embargo on American ships was very damaging, and while the new *Maximum* taxing grain profits might have the advantage of discouraging speculation and inflation at home, it restricted foreign trade by eating into profits. The Republic must realize that international trade was not a philanthropic exercise. Fenwick then raised some specific questions: if the Republic failed to buy the entire cargo of a ship, who would pay for the rest? Consider for example the case of a merchant-captain who arrives from the United States with a shipload of rice and tobacco, and suppose that the Republic buys all the rice but only half the tobacco and pays for the transaction in wine. To what port can the ship go with a cargo of Bordeaux wine and American tobacco when the importation of French wine is forbidden in Spain and England?

Fenwick was clever at dealing with the French authorities in Bordeaux even as the Terror was being introduced into the *département* by two Convention envoys—Ysabeau and Tallien. For the most part, however, Fenwick and the other Americans were in these men's good graces, and when Bordeaux celebrated the recapture of Toulon, the two Frenchmen included the following details in their report of the ceremony to the Committee of Public Safety:

> More than two hundred of our American brothers joined us in the celebration, carrying the flags of both our countries. Citizen Fenwick, the United States consul, sat with us on the platform in the Temple of Reason and he gave a brief and touching speech on the union of our two republics. The fraternal accolade that greeted his speech was heartwarming to behold.

By the end of 1793, the few English subjects Mary Wollstonecraft counted among her friends had disappeared from the Paris scene: the Christies had returned to London and Miss Williams was awaiting better days in Basel. So when her lover, Gilbert Imlay, found himself spending more and more time at Le Havre on business, she decided to join him there. Imlay's only interest now was money—how to apply his intelligence to business and his imagination to profits, for he was determined to make a fortune.

The couple settled in a working-class neighborhood where they rented part of a house belonging to the Wheatcrofts' son. The Wheatcroft family made soap in Le Havre–Marat. As Mary was expecting her baby in May, Wheatcroft and his wife—although a very correct, bourgeois pair—went out of their way to help with the move and found them a pearl of a servant named Marguerite.

The birth of little Fanny brought joy to the entire house, and Marguerite could not do enough for mother and child.

The home on the rue de la Corderie, however, was hardly a calm refuge. Driven by ambition, Imlay was playing with fire and it often made him gloomy. His contacts were almost entirely with traffickers and seafarers on the lookout for windfalls. Their only interest was money and they talked business from morning until night. Mary found their sordid materialism revolting and longed for the philosophical discussions she used to have with writers and artists at Joseph Johnson's in London, for the lively hours in Paris where the conversation dealt with the subject of happiness, the liberation of women, the latest speeches at the Club des Jacobins, the newest patriotic poetry or play, or the Salon and David's most recent entry. Imperceptibly, she began to realize that her companion was a grasping man, greedy for a wealth she despised. Unable to restrain her contempt, she either ridiculed Imlay's visitors or expressed her disapproval with silence. By contrast, she saw herself as a pure spirit blessed with sensibility, love, and maternity, who was concerned only with ideas.

The worst of it was that Imlay's transactions paid poorly and the household lived on the edge of poverty. When Robespierre's fall brought about a change in the economy and opened up new fields for speculation, Imlay decided to abandon his field of operations in Le Havre and move to a more active marketplace. He would try London first, then return to Paris, so he settled Mary, Fanny, and Marguerite in the French capital to wait for his return.

Mary tried to keep her illusions, and Imlay wrote her cajoling letters to sustain her faith and allay her impatience. At first, Mary answered in kind. She had met Rouget de Lisle, creator of *La Marseillaise*, and wrote to her fickle friend that if he did not return soon, she might fall in love with the composer, who also played the violin divinely even though his handsome face was a bit overblown.

With time, her letters became less playful. She wrote him about a German lady she had met while walking Fanny, the lady having a child of the same age. Mary was full of admiration for her new friend because she was entirely responsible for her own life and that of her child. "I envy her," Mary wrote to Imlay.

Imlay had given her a letter of credit against funds he had on deposit in Paris. She made two withdrawals, then determined to support herself in spite of her loathing for all commercial activity. But material difficulties soon caught up with her, and, consumed with a desire to see her faithless friend, Mary crossed the Channel to track him down.

She found him installed with a new love and, in her despair, Mary threw herself into the Thames from Putney Bridge. But the river rejected the forsaken woman and she was forced to accept her fate and remain among the living.

Contrary to popular songs, love's pain lasts no longer than love's pleasure. Mary formed a new attachment to William Godwin, and a second pregnancy followed—fatal in this instance, for Mary died while giving birth to the girl who was to join her life to Shelley's stormy existence.


By the late winter of 1794, the food crisis had worsened, discontent increased, and the various factions grown more suspicious of each other. Then the scandal of the *Compagnie des Indes* exploded. The poet-philospher Fabre d'Eglantine was sucked into the scandal, and he in turn brought down Camille Desmoulins. With them fell Danton. Their backs to the wall, the perpetrators denounced each other, and the

Paris Commune's mouthpiece, Hébert, used his salacious sheet *Père Duchesne* to call for more and more heads.*

Robespierre, believing that the two extremes—Danton's *Indulgents* and Hébert's *Enragés*—were no better than "brigands in a forest," decided to strike alternatively against both sides. The arrest, trial, and execution of Hébert and his followers ensued, and soon after, that of Danton and his supporters.

Lying side by side in the hecatomb with the French traitors were alleged foreign agents such as the Prussian Baron Cloots, victim of his own aberrations (among them, proclaiming himself Ambassador of the Human Race), and the two Austrian Barons Frey, victims of their excessive avarice. The guillotine put an end to many a financial transaction, including those of the Dutch banker Kock, the Austrian Berchtold Proli, the Castillian Guzman, and the Portuguese Pereira. Most of the financiers based in Brussels and Geneva escaped the net, and the British banker Walter Boyd got back to England unharmed. Of the foreign merchants, not a single American was touched: they were far too circumspect to venture onto dangerous political ground. They gauged the mood of the country from their daily

---

* The *Compagnie des Indes* scandal, in terms of the corrupt use of government machinery, was on a par with America's Teapot Dome affair. Many in Danton's circle committed fraud and larceny, using their positions within the Convention and the committees to gain personal wealth at the expense of the nation. But underlying the three-way fight among Danton, Robespierre, and Hébert was also a disagreement over the Terror. For Robespierre, to whom honesty and hard work were high virtues, the Terror was merely a means of discipline. For the Dantonists, entrepreneurial in outlook, it was at best a bother and at worst a menace to their personal aggrandizement. To the men in Hébert's group, it was the supreme device for implementing their rhetoric.

contacts with its people. They heard them inveigh against the merchants and the rich; they saw their grievances spread across newspapers and seditious posters on the walls. Everything pointed to imminent insurrection.

Major Jackson's efforts on behalf of Thomas Paine did not prevent him from carrying out his mission for William Bingham. He appeared before the Committee of Public Safety to propose that France buy two million acres of American forest land belonging to Bingham. The land, in the area of the Saint Lawrence River, was rich in a variety of resources, including lumber for the navy yards of France and her colonies.

Jackson was dealing with hardened realists; the people's representatives listened attentively, weighed the pros and cons, and carefully examined the figures. In the end, they declined the offer because such an operation would bleed France of its wealth. It made little sense to dispose of the nation's assets in France in order to use them in America, thereby holding enormous reserves of exotic woods on the far side of the Atlantic whose exploitation would have the added disadvantage of encouraging emigration. Such a deal would result in a loss of men and money at the very moment when the Republic had urgent need of all its children and all its resources. Jackson saw that it was useless to press the matter further, and the meeting ended with expressions of mutual esteem.

Bingham's agent had good reason to feel scant affection for a country that had assaulted him on his arrival, that treated Thomas Paine with indignity, and whose Committee of Public Safety had just turned down his proposition. In spite of these adverse elements, however, Jackson's admiration for

231

its people and institutions continued unabated. Although his work was done, he could not tear himself away. On his first visit, Versailles's gilt had left him unmoved, and he had applauded the demise of the Ancien Régime and its pomp. Now fate willed that, having seen the excesses of royalty, he would return to France to witness those of its people. In London, where everyone dwelt on the excesses, he had listened to Englishmen and French émigrés outdo each other on the atrocities, telling how the butchers' lockers in Paris were plentifully stocked with human flesh fresh from the guillotine.

But now that he was seeing the Revolution with his own eyes, he became its fervent partisan. To be sure, he had witnessed many an execution, yet he never thought of the guillotine as a symbol of the revolutionary regime. He was taken with the Revolution's promises of a better life rather than its machine of death, and saw many grounds for hope around him. Disregarding the melodrama and imagery of events, he concentrated on the Republic's efforts at organization. Besides, France's patriotic ardor fascinated him.

He looked, listened, informed himself, read, and took notes. After three months in a France mobilized for total war, he put his observations down on paper and sent them to his friend Rufus King, now United States minister in London. He marveled at what an energetic race these Frenchmen were, at their vigorous potential, even in the gentler sex. While London was talking about *tricoteuses,* Jackson chose to overlook this negligible fraction of the female population, seeing only the anonymous mass of heroines doing men's work—like caryatids holding up the edifice while their men were away at war.

Side by side with the women, he went on, the old people

and children worked the soil and grew vegetables "by a late refinement in chemistry." Even the gardens of the Tuileries were under cultivation, and what satisfaction to see the potato given a place of honor, its virtues finally recognized!

What a country! France was resisting on all fronts: at the same time that it was fighting a foreign coalition and internal sedition, it was transforming the former palace of its kings into a national museum "whose richness exceeds any other collection in Europe." Reigning over the vegetable gardens in its park, the Louvre had become a repository of fine art, while on the other side of the Seine, the Gobelins continued to weave "the most exquisite productions of the needle and shuttle."

Of all the products of French genius, Jackson gave first place to its military organization. Every man between the ages of eighteen and twenty-five was under arms; all metallurgists had been requisitioned to make war supplies while that part of the population unable to bear arms produced saltpeter "in incredible amounts. Wherever you move, or to whatever quarter your attention is turned, nothing meets the view but warlike preparations. Every consideration is sacrificed to public exigence, every contribution of property or service, which the public necessity requires, appears to be cheerfully made."

Pen in hand, he figured the republican forces at 1.2 million men, "exceeding in numbers and array all that the world has hitherto exhibited." The army of the north alone was 254,000 strong. And all these soldiers marched with precision; after the relaxation of discipline during the last year of the monarchy, rigorous order was now back in force.

This marvelous instrument, blessed with its incomparable cavalry and unequaled artillery, led Major Jackson to make a prophetic statement: "A Nation of 28 millions of people, situated as France is, being compelled to become a nation of Soldiers, should, within a very short period, achieve whatever conquest they attempt." And, Jackson added, "In the course of conquest it is to be feared that the lust of dominion may lead this People, already the Happiest Nation on the globe in geographical position, to grasp at possessions, which, far from increasing, would eventually abridge both their happiness and their power."

He went on to explain that credit for the Republic's organization must go to the Convention and its committees, with the Committee of Public Safety the mainspring that set everything in motion. "Certainly Robespierre is the apex of this pyramid," and in Jackson's view, Danton's disappearance and the extinction of Hébert and his party were simple political operations designed to ensure the stability of power within the logic dictated by events. Once the place was cleaned out and the followers of Danton and Hébert eliminated, there was nothing to stop the nation from rising to new heights. Military victories would follow, and at last the people would be able to enjoy the fruits of the Revolution.

Gouverneur Morris' cleverness and Genêt's clumsiness had brought both men to a dead end, forcing their two governments to demand their recall. Both men complied with equally poor grace.

Morris had excused his lack of hurry on the grounds that he wanted to wait for his successor so that the post would not be left empty. However, once James Monroe did arrive, Morris waited another three months before leaving, and even then he did not return to America but moved to Switzerland where he could watch the situation evolve from close at hand.

Meanwhile, the Terror was interfering with his habitual way of life, and he had to spend most of his time at his pretty house at Seine-Port, leaving behind two assistants to manage the legation's business. To keep him abreast of their activities, they shuttled between rue de la Planche and Morris' country house.

One of the two was Henry Walter Livingston, a New Yorker who had been the minister's secretary for a year. A young lawyer barely twenty-five years of age, he made regular trips to London to make sure that official dispatches destined for the United States were safe from the prying eyes of the British "black Cabinet." The second assistant was Major James Cole Mountflorence, a former officer who served as chancellor of the legation. It was he who had stood in for Morris at Admiral John Paul Jones's funeral.

Morris rarely went to Paris, for he risked having his carriage stopped, his identity checked, as well as insolent requests made for his papers. One day he was stopped in the street, and, as he did not have the proper "civic card," he was forced to appear before the officials of Butte-les-Moulins even though he was the United States minister. As soon as he was released, he lost no time protesting this irregularity and was immediately given a passport that allowed him to move freely throughout the Republic.

With the dissolution of the court, he had curbed his political intrigues, and although he was still well informed, he did not let it show. He prudently kept his knowledge to himself, not even sharing it with his diary. He wrote only the most prosaic letters, in which he described the view from his windows at Seine-Port, one looking out on the ruins of baths purportedly used by Gabrielle, Henri IV's mistress, another, the pavilion of Croix-Fontaine, built for Louis XV by *Fermier-Général* Bouret, Adélaïde de Flahaut's natural father. Morris, who had an insatiable appetite for luxury, noted the fact that Bouret had spent more than twelve million francs on its construction and the surrounding gardens.

In May 1793, the American minister received a visit from an emissary of Mme. de Lafayette. The marquis was imprisoned in Austria; the marquise had just been arrested in the Auvergne and was about to be taken to Paris for her imprisonment, leaving behind her daughters and son—George Washington's godson. She had begged Frestel, the young boy's tutor, to escort her as far as Melun, then leave her to go visit Gouverneur Morris and inform him of her family's predicament and need for help. Specifically, she wanted her son to go to America so that he could be under his godfather's protection.

Morris and Frestel discussed the possibilities of an appeal to the French government. The American was not against trying, but the ambiguity of his position had rendered his credit of little value. On the other hand, he still had a fat purse, and he straightway gave his visitor enough money to alleviate the prisoner's captivity and provide aid to her children.

Meanwhile, the Vicomtesse de Damas had been looking for a safe retreat, and she soon found one with Morris at Seine-Port. So far the young woman had known only the worldly courtier side of the American minister, but she was soon amazed to find that he was equally a lover of nature. She once described Morris' principal character trait thus: "In his view, you carry out the orders of Providence by enjoying all your faculties: to enjoy is to obey."

During that beautiful summer of 1793, Mme. de Damas watched him tending his farm and gardens, and together they enjoyed the produce of his barn and courtyard, vegetable garden and orchard. She was surprised to find that the American seemed "much happier among the simple village folk of Seine-Port than he had ever been in the brilliant circles of Versailles and Paris." In point of fact, his relationship with the "simple villagers" was larded with many a voluptuous hour of relaxation.

In November, the police knocked on the door of Mme. de Damas's mother, the Comtesse de Langeron in Paris, and that lady was forced to admit that her daughter, "Citizeness Langeron, wife Damas" was staying with the United States minister at Seine-Port. Morris tried to mollify the police by saying that he would answer for his guest, but he struck them as a poor guarantor. Indifferent to his protestations, they took the lady off to prison.

As the tempest tossed people about, sending some into exile, to prison, or to the scaffold, others were plagued with only petty annoyances. The Revolutionary Tribunal may have eclipsed all other jurisdictions, but the justices of the peace continued to deal with minor offenses in their time-honored way.

In normal times, the United States minister to France would never have entertained the possibility that he might one day become involved with a little country judge. His only relationship with the justice of the peace in Boisette, the small neighboring town to his country place, had been limited to an exchange of nods. When the minister's carriage passed by, Citizen Cartault stood rigidly by the side of the road, bonnet in hand, while the other gave a lordly wave through the window.

Now, a theft of jewels took place at Seine-Port in the home of the man who was deferentially known in the region as "the American ambassador," and it was with considerable emotion that Citizen Cartault opened the investigation. His eyes must have popped at the list of missing jewels—ornaments for the hair, for the neck, belts, shoes, earrings of every description, necklaces, bracelets, diamond buttons, gold boxes for beauty patches and toothpicks, candy boxes, snuffboxes inlaid with precious stones, watches set with pearls, chains and medallions, one of which carried the inscription: "To my beautiful Sofie." This last bauble belonged to "Citizeness Demory" (or Demaury), who lived at Gouverneur Morris', and the theft was discovered when Julie, that lady's maid, left her employ. Through a coincidence that gave rise to a good deal of speculation, at the same moment, another maid, Geneviève, reached Paris with a trunk that was assumed to contain the jewels. Or at least that is the impression Mlle. Demory wanted to give. The justice of the peace had Julie arrested along with her friend l'Epine, Morris' valet, and the two were locked up locally. At the same time, he put the Paris police on Geneviève's traces.

Preferring easy solutions, Paris magistrates were inclined to suspect servants. They found the maid and took possession of the trunk as soon as the riverboat reached the port of Saint-Paul. Their search discovered nothing. So they had to post the following notice on the walls of Paris:

IMPORTANT NOTICE: Stolen: about one hundred thousand francs' worth of diamonds and jewels from the home of the Minister Plenipotentiary of the United States of America at Seine-Port in the district of Melun.

All citizens, jewelers, and watchmakers and any others as well as pawnbrokers and commission agents are asked to arrest any one possessing these stolen objects and so inform the minister and Citizen Cartault, justice of the peace in Boisette, near Melun.

The town of Boisette and its environs took a passionate interest in the great jewel robbery. Boisette and Seine-Port finally had their own scandal, and a juicy one at that, with an American tang to lend it savor. Everyone in the cast was a familiar figure: the minister with the wooden leg who was a devotee of agriculture, Mlle. Demory and her furbelows, Geneviève and Julie and l'Epine, the last a stage valet to end all valets except that he enjoyed an occasional glass of wine with the boys in the village.

The idea started with the humble folk, then spread to other levels of society. Tongues began to wag: so they were looking for a wicked girl? Well, no need to go looking for her in Paris, no need even to leave the house. Mlle. Demory did not enjoy the best of reputations, and was explicitly accused of "having robbed herself." Although this astonished the justice of the peace, he thought it wise to include the hypothesis in his report to his superiors, stating that the lady was quite capable of such a subterfuge "to get even with the respectable man at whose house the theft was committed."

With the Terror in full swing, a false step could cost the justice dear, and Citizen Cartault was indeed in a tight spot: the minister was quite capable of flying off the handle, declaring the tramp innocent, and handing over to Fouquier-Tinville the task of clearing up Citizen Cartault's insinuations. But the "respectable man" did nothing; he was embarrassed by the scandal and not especially flattered to see his name posted on all the walls of Paris in connection with a theft of diamonds. As luck would have it, a few days later, on

July 9, the last whiff of scandal was dissipated, together with Robespierre's regime.

That was Gouverneur Morris' last claim to the capital's attention. His successor, James Monroe, soon arrived, and Morris turned over the legation and his *hôtel* on the rue de la Planche to him. A few months later, he took off for Switzerland—after one last night of love that left him "with strong emotion which affects me much." His companion of the moment, one Mme. Simon whom he had met at a dinner given by the banker Greffulhe at the time of Louis XVI's trial, had come down from Paris to lend enchantment to his last night at Seine-Port. Before separating, the lovers made plans for a reunion in Switzerland, and they met in Hamburg as well the following spring.

The dashing diplomat was much taken with the pretty émigré who was looking for "a convenient means of cuckolding her husband," as he put it in his diary. He also noted that to make better use of her time in exile, Mme. Simon had formed "a Lesbian attachment to Mlle. Renault, the mistress of Walkier." No longer fearing the revolutionary police or its prying into his papers, Morris had returned to his earlier freedom of expression.

While the Imlay household was still living at Le Havre–Marat, an American merchant named William Vans settled there as well. Vans had spent his early youth on the high seas in the employ of a Salem trader, and thanks to the profits realized in the spice and gold trades, the enterprising young man had managed to charter his own ship. Together with another American, he founded the firm of Freeman and Vans.

He was barely thirty when his travels happened to take him to London. It was then 1793 and the French Revolution and its effect on trade were on everyone's lips. He listened, discussed, assessed which way the wind was blowing, learned exactly the nature of France's needs, then launched his operation. Returning to the United States, he fitted out a ship, took on the required merchandise, and set sail. After successfully maneuvering around the privateers, he made a safe landing at Le Havre. He immediately sold his entire cargo with a 50 percent profit. On the strength of this transaction, the firm of Freeman and Vans organized a veritable armada that shuttled back and forth across the Atlantic with profits always ahead of losses. To be sure, on its way to Bordeaux to pick up merchandise that Fenwick, the consul, had assembled, the brig *Sally Ann* was picked up by the British, but that was one of the risks of the trade, and Vans was not overly disturbed.

A certain merchant in Le Havre, Guillaume Michel Gauvain, greatly admired Vans's flotilla. When he saw the *David*, the *Margarita*, the *Lucy*, the *Tethis*, the *Jefferson*, or the *Governor Bowdoin* emptying their cornucopias on the docks of Le Havre, he congratulated himself on his good relations with the dispenser of such riches. Their business relationship soon ripened into friendship, and when the American was invited to the Gauvains' home, he found himself much taken with their daughter, Céleste Rosalie, a fresh young girl of nineteen. On her side, the young lady liked the foreigner's ways, which betokened the glamour of America and Paris. The capital being the Republic's chief marketplace, Vans naturally spent much time there. When he returned to Le Havre, he always brought back a stock of anecdotes as well as orders, and the Gauvain family was much impressed. He would talk about the Palais Egalité, his countrymen, the shops, the restaurants, the cafés and theaters.

At the mention of the word "marriage," M. Gauvain was placed in a quandary. To be sure, his daughter's young admirer had a brilliant nose for business and was indeed prosperous, but the father had no idea of his background, and the head of a respectable family could hardly give his daughter's hand in marriage without certain guarantees. Vans set out to collect testimonials, but since most of these were written in English, it necessitated a sworn interpreter.

Citizen Bernier, official translator for Le Havre–Marat, was able to satisfy all scruples: William Vans was a legitimate child, born in Boston, thirty-one years of age, had never been married before, and therefore nothing stood in the way of his union with Céleste Rosalie Gauvain.

The conjugal preliminaries followed, and the sworn interpreter gave way to the notary. What a to-do to enter into a simple thing like marriage in the land of the Rights of Man! The New World was still tainted with a hint of the barbarian, it paid little heed to Roman tradition, and young people contracted marriages without a thought to the price of butter or what the future might hold. They went into it gaily with their eyes closed, oblivious to any need for assurances. But the French Republic had not abandoned the monarchy's legacy of lawyers with their jargon and fine print. One didn't set off for the Temple of Venus without a sou in one's pocket. In a notary's eyes, lovers were reduced to litigants in a business deal, for there must be provisions for the signatories to file a complaint should the day arrive when one or the other felt constrained by the bargain. The Revolution may have scrapped all religious ceremonies, but although it had dispensed with the Church, it had not dared touch the

242

pocketbook. Thus the notary's marriage contract listed what the future bride would bring to the union: first, what money; second, what furniture; third, her trousseau, with the value of each item translated into *écus*. Then, the groom had to indicate how he proposed to contribute to the financial resources of the household. When it came to clothing, the notary demanded an estimate of its worth. Vans had to count up his trousers and place a value on them. But that wasn't all: the American was introduced to the demands of "Normandy customs," which required him to guarantee his fiancée a permanent income.

While the men dickered over the negotiations, Céleste Rosalie put the finishing touches to her trousseau and dreamed of Paris, where she was sure to lead a far pleasanter life than she had in Le Havre–Marat. Still carefree and foolish like most young people, she gave little attention to the reports of tragic events, which in any event were glossed over by middle-class families or even disregarded. The outcry of starving peasants did not reach the ears of comfortable bourgeois children, and their parents saw to it that they were well protected from reality.

The marriage took place in the Parish House of Le Havre–Marat. Jean-Baptiste Boucherot, public official for the second *arrondissement*, performed the formalities in the name of the law and declared the couple united in marriage, in accordance with the laws of the Republic then in force. Once married, William Vans kept to his promise and took his bride to Paris, where they moved into a furnished house near the Palais Egalité—a district full of possibilities where one could get rich on the rue Vivienne and lose it all in the gaming houses that proliferated in the neighborhood.

The young couple began to circulate about Paris like true

natives. As if to spite the Terror, the city still offered many pleasures. Shaking the provincial dust off their feet, the newlyweds threw themselves avidly into every form of frivolity.

A month went by, July 9 arrived, and it would have been like any other day but for the fact that Vans had agreed to be a witness at a fellow American's marriage that day. The ceremony, identical to the one in which Vans had starred a few weeks earlier, took place in an attractive and bustling town hall. The municipal officer pronounced the sacramental words, the couple exchanged vows and rings, then signed the civil register, their witnesses following suit. The wedding party walked to the Place de Grève, stepped into a hackney coach, and rode off to the ritual feast.

It was hot. As the heat of the day gave way to a torrid evening, a pervasive sound broke the evening stillness: Paris was making itself heard. Tocsin and cannon joined in to punctuate the people's cheers. Something of great moment had just occurred: the Convention had vomited its Committee of Public Safety.

Robespierre and his followers, rescued from their enemies by the still-loyal forces of the Commune, suddenly appeared in the Place de Grève and headed for the town hall now lit by torches. The very room where the young couple had pronounced their timid vows now provided the stage for a settlement of accounts and noisy harangues. Barras arrived unexpectedly, sword held high, his troops at his heels. There was an exchange of shots, and a body fell from a window and crashed onto the pavement like a disjointed puppet. The municipal employees, so proper in the exercise of their functions a moment before, scattered like a flight of swallows as blood spattered the formal rooms, even staining the civil register.

244

Robespierre, his jaw broken, was left writhing in agony; his partner in the triumvirate, Couthon, who had been shoved down the stairs in his wheelchair, lay panting in its wreckage until morning.

Meanwhile, the newspapers were preparing their morning editions and the goosequills boldly spelled out the vengeful new adjective "infamous," which would thereafter attach itself to Robespierre's name, replacing the erstwhile "incorruptible."

# Epilogue

JAMES MONROE, SUCCEEDING GOUVERNEUR MORRIS AS MINISTER to France just after the collapse of the Reign of Terror, saw the ship of state turned over to the doubtful captaincies of Tallien and Barras.

Little was known of these two men, although the name Barras was familiar to American ears through his uncle, Admiral de Barras, who distinguished himself during the War of Independence, and was portrayed standing between Lafayette and Rochambeau in Trumbull's painting of the surrender of Cornwallis at Yorktown.

His nephew, however, enjoyed a far less glorious reputation; a former nobleman and officer in the King's armies who had passed over to the revolutionary side, he was known as a corrupt intriguer, and it was whispered that if he conspired to bring down Robespierre, it was to seize the initiative before the Incorruptible One could do the same to him.

In spite of the poor reputation of the new leaders, the change was generally welcome. It promised the sorely needed restoration of liberty, not only the liberty of those suspects in prison, but liberty in every domain, including a return to freedom in the marketplace, which had been so woefully restricted by the recent laws.

Even so, the prisons were slow to release their inmates, and the reasons given were ambiguous at best. The Marquis de Sade was quickly back in circulation because his morals in no way troubled the men in power; on the other hand, no effort was made to liberate such inoffensive prisoners as the two Duchesses de La Rochefoucauld, Thomas Paine, and the Marquise de Lafayette. James Monroe spent several months trying to obtain the release of the last two and finally succeeded after long delays. But for all William Short's impassioned pleas from Madrid, Monroe refused to dilute his efforts by helping the French ladies. Better that he should use his influence for the benefit of Thomas Paine and Mme. de Lafayette, for they meant far more to the people of the United States.

When Thomas Paine was at long last released from Luxembourg prison, he was in such a sad state that James Monroe and his wife Eliza offered to care for him in their own home. They called in Dr. Desault, the best doctor in Paris, who had taken care of Louis XVI's son up to the time of his death. Desault worked wonders, and in no time the invalid was back on his feet.

But Paine's trials had been too much for him. Soured by his experience, the old pamphleteer had lost his spark along with his illusions, and he used what energies he had left to attack George Washington for not lifting a finger in his behalf. Monroe tried to counsel moderation, but in the end he had to sever the relationship. Paine stayed on in Paris until 1802. When he returned to America, it was to find that he was as unpopular then as he had been idolized before. He died a miserable death, comforted only by the ministrations of Mme. de Bonneville, the widow of his Paris printer, who had crossed the Atlantic with him.

Nor was William Short's return to America a happy one. Rebuffs and disappointments were to dog him the rest of his days. When Jefferson appointed him minister to Russia in 1808, he reached Paris only to learn that the Senate had voted against his appointment on the pretext that a permanent representative in Russia was not called for. Short profited from his stay in Paris to plead his case once again with his beloved Rosalie, but to no avail. Perhaps both were fated to live joyless lives, or perhaps she had been turning him down for so long—albeit with a heavy heart—that she found it impossible to break the habit. Short returned to America alone, but their correspondence continued for another quarter-century, even after her marriage to the Comte de Castellane. Short settled in Philadelphia, and with the fruits from his cultivation of Dutch bankers, he was able to buy extensive lands in Kentucky and northern New York.

By a curious quirk of fate, both Citizen Genêt and Gouverneur Morris ended their lives as gentlemen farmers in New York State. The resilient Genêt, unabashed by his repudiation by Washington, carved out an exemplary and many-faceted life in his adopted country. He married Cornelia Tappen Clinton, daughter of the then governor of New York, and moved to a farm in Rensselaer County where he devoted himself to the technical problems confronting the young republic. His interests ranged from agriculture to science and mechanics, and he wrote variously on public health, "the upper forces of fluids and their applicability to several arts," and the growth and manufacture of silk, not to mention a brief supporting the election of his father-in-law to the Presidency of the United States.

For Morris, his post in Paris was his last diplomatic assignment; perhaps his unsavory reputation had finally caught up with him. On his belated return to the United States, he did serve as Senator from New York for three years, but spent the rest of his life on his estate in Gouverneur, New York. He finally even married: at the age of fifty-seven, he took Anne Cary Randolph of Virginia as his wife. They had a son, and it was his great-granddaughter, Beatrice Cary Davenport, who brought out his extraordinary diary in 1932.

As for his lady love, the mettlesome Adélaïde, when her husband was guillotined for his part in the importation of counterfeit *assignats* from Britain to depreciate French money, the widow decided to reestablish her position with a brilliant marriage. She first set her trap in England, then in Switzerland; finally she fixed her eye on a Portuguese diplomat. To the Comte de Souza-Bothelo, she played the virtuous widow beset with misfortunes and torn from her happy home by the revolutionary tides. She won the man and the title of Madame Ambassador into the bargain.

For Joel Barlow, the end of the Revolution served only to increase his diplomatic and literary involvements. In 1795 David Humphreys had him appointed consul in Algiers to see what he could do to solve the still vexing problem of the captive American sailors. Once the ransom was agreed upon, Barlow had to use all his skills to temporize with the terrible Dey of Algiers as he waited for the money to arrive. In the end, he was so successful that he was able to return to Paris, having concluded three treaties permitting American ships in the Mediterranean, one with the Dey, another with the Bey of Tunis, and a third with the Pasha of Tripoli. There followed several years of writing poetry and essays on political, economic, and scientific questions. He also went into partnership with Robert Fulton in the testing and promotion of Fulton's steam engines, their experiments roiling the waters of the Seine as they would later the Potomac and the Hudson.

The Barlows returned to America in 1805, and thanks to their investments in French consols, they were able to buy a handsome estate near Washington, which they christened Kalorama ("fine view" in Greek) and where Jefferson and Madison often came to visit.

But Joel Barlow was not done with France. In 1811, Madison appointed him minister to France with instructions to negotiate commercial treaties with Napoleon. The timing was unfortunate. Barlow had to chase the French Emperor across the frozen reaches of Europe to Russia, missed him in Moscow, and headed for Wilno in Poland where Napoleon was expected next. His wit still intact and his love for his wife undiminished, he wrote her from Wilno: "I love my darling, first begotten, long-beloved wife better & more & harder & softer & longer & stronger than all the Poles between the south pole and the north pole." When Napoleon was defeated at Beresina, Barlow started back to Paris. But he caught a chill on the way that developed into pneumonia, and he died in Zarnowiec, a small village near Krakow where he still lies buried, a Connecticut Yankee in distant Poland.

# Bibliographic Notes

## CHAPTER 1

For this and subsequent chapters, see *The Papers of Thomas Jefferson*, Julian Boyd et al., eds., Princeton, N.J., 1950. 19 vols. as of 1974.

On the Langeac Hotel: Howard C. Rice, *L'Hôtel de Langeac*, Paris, 1947.

On Lafayette: *Mémoires, Correspondance et Manuscrits du général La Fayette*, Paris, 1838.

On the redemption of the American sailors: H. G. Barnby, *The Prisoners of Algiers*, Oxford, 1966.

On William Langborn: C. C. Davis, "The Curious Colonel Langborn," in the *Virginia Magazine of History*, October 1956.

On William Short: unedited papers in the Library of Congress, the Pennsylvania Historical Society, and the Philosophical Society of Philadelphia; Yvon Bizardel and Howard C. Rice, "Poor in Love Mr. Short," *The William and Mary Quarterly*, 1964.

On John Trumbull: *Autobiography*, Theodore Sizer, ed., New Haven, Conn., 1958; Yvon Bizardel, *American Painters in Paris*, New York, 1960.

On Gouverneur Morris in this and subsequent chapters: the principal source is his journal, *A Diary of the French Revolution*, Beatrice Cary Davenport, ed., Boston, 1932; also, Howard Swiggett, *The Extraordinary Mr. Morris*, Garden City, L.I., 1952.

On George Schaffner and the Marquis de La Roüerie: "George Schaffner," in the *Bulletin of the Lancaster County Historical Society*, 1946; Chateaubriand, *Mémoires d'Outre-Tombe*, 1950; G. Lenotre, *Le Marquis de La Roüerie et la conjuration bretonne*, 1899. On La Roüerie's imprisonment in the Bastille, Police Department records, July–September 1788.

On Joel Barlow: the *Barlow Papers*, Houghton Library, Harvard University; James Woodress, *A Yankee's Odyssey, The Life of Joel Barlow*, Philadelphia, 1958.

## CHAPTER 2

As a general reference, see Jean Bouchary, *Les Compagnies financières à Paris à la fin du XVIII<sup>e</sup> siècle*, Vol. 3, Paris, 1942; also, an anonymous pamphlet, "Avis à ceux qui voudraient aller en Amérique," published by Benjamin Franklin, Passy, 1784. Jacques Ragondez's letter appears in *Jefferson Papers*, Vol. 14.

On Mme. de Tessé: A. Callet, *Anne-Paule-Dominique de Noailles, Marquise de Montagu*, Paris, 1864; Antonin de Mun, *Claude Adrien de Mun, sa vie et son temps*, Paris, 1962; Yvon Bizardel, *Une amie française de Jefferson, la comtesse de Tessé*, Friends of the Blérancourt Museum, Paris, 1965.

On the Mirabeau incident: the transcripts of the Assembly, July 1789, and *Le Moniteur* of the same month; Aulard, "La Dette américaine envers la France," in *La Revue de Paris*, May and June 1925.

On Mme. de Flahaut (later the Marquise de Souza-Bothelo): in addition to Gouverneur Morris' *Diary*, see Saint-Beuve, *Portraits de femmes*, 1834; André de Maricourt, *Madame de Souza et sa famille*, 1913.

## CHAPTER 3

On Mme. de Corny: Gilbert Chinard, *Trois amitiés françaises de Jefferson*, 1927.

On the Scioto Company: in addition to Bouchary, *Les Compagnies financières* (cited for Chapter 2), see J. J. Belote, *The Scioto Speculation*, Cincinnati, 1907; also, pertinent documents in the Municipal Archives in Le Havre.

On Ruth Barlow: the *Barlow Papers* (cited above, for Chapter 1); also, the *Baldwin Papers*, Henry E. Huntington Library, San Marino, Calif.

On the American sailors held in Algiers: E. Dupuy, *Américains et Barbaresques*, Paris, 1910.

On Thomas Paine: Daniel Conway, *The Life of Thomas Paine*, London, 1909; A. O. Aldridge, *Man of Reason, The Life of Thomas Paine*, Philadelphia, 1959; and Albert Mathiez, *La Révolution et les étrangers*.

On John Paul Jones: Samuel Eliot Morison, *John Paul Jones, A Sailor's Biography*, Boston, 1959; Joseph Conway, *Footprints of Famous Americans in Paris*, London, 1912.

On the celebration of the Federation: the transcripts of the July 10, 1790, session of the National Assembly, and the issue of *Le Moniteur* in which the session is covered.

On W. H. Vernon: his speech before the July 10, 1790, session of the National Assembly on the behalf of the American citizens, Bibliothèque Nationale.

On Colonel Benjamin Walker: E. S. Whitely, *Washington and His Aides*, New York, 1936.

## CHAPTER 4

On the Nantucket whalers: the transcripts of the January 24, 1791, session of the National Assembly.

On Lewis Littlepage: C. C. Davis, *The King's Chevalier, A Biography of Lewis Littlepage*, 1961; Lewis Littlepage, *Private and Political Memoirs*, ed., C. C. Davis, American Philosophical Society, 1957; Edmund Burke, *Reflections on the Revolution in France*, London, 1790.

On the address to the French people by Achille Duchastellet: the transcripts of the July 1, 1791, session of the National Assembly; also, Etienne Dumont, *Souvenirs sur Mirabeau*.

On Duchastellet: David de Saint-Georges, "Achille François de Lascaris d'Urfé Marquis du Chastellet," in *Biographies foréziennes*, Dijon, 1896.

## CHAPTER 5

The lease for Gouverneur Morris' occupancy of the Hôtel Seymour is in the National Archives.

On John Skey Eustace: see his personal letters and pamphlets in the British Museum and Bibliothèque Nationale. His dossier as an officer in the French army is preserved in the army's Historical Archives at Vincennes.

The nomination of George Schaffner as adjutant-general in the Breton army is included in Calonne's papers, in the Public Record Office in London. Both the events during Whitsuntide, 1792, at the Château de La Roüerie as well as Schaffner's arrest and interrogation are recounted in the transcripts in the National Archives.

## CHAPTER 6

For the correspondence between Gouverneur Morris and Lebrun-Tondu, see the Archives of the Minister of Foreign Affairs.

On the death and funeral of John Paul Jones, see the *Communication de la commission du Vieux Paris,* Paris, Imprimerie Municipale, 1906.

On the banquet at the Hôtel White: see both *Le Patriote français,* December 1792–January 1793, and the pamphlet "Adresse des Anglois," taken from the transcripts of the November 20, 1792, session of the Convention, Bibliothèque Nationale.

## CHAPTER 7

On Genêt: Mme. Roland, *Mémoires;* the Executive Council, *Mémoire pour servir à L'introduction du citoyen Genêt,* Paris, December 1792, in the Archives of the Minister of Foreign Affairs; and Mangourit's papers in the District Archives of Sion, Switzerland.

For general information on France's plans regarding Louisiana, see several documents published by *The American Historical Review* in 1898 and in April 1924; also, the *American State Papers,* Vol. 39, Washington, D.C.

On General Clark: John Bakeless, *Background to Glory, The Life of George Rogers Clark,* Philadelphia, 1957.

On Thomas Paine and the decision regarding the fate of Louis XVI: the transcripts of the Convention, January 15 and 19, 1793, and February 1, 1793.

## CHAPTER 8

On Mrs. Williams and her daughters: Funck-Brentano's preface to the reedition of Miss Williams' *Mémoires;* Lionel D. Woodward, *An English Friend of the French Revolution, Miss H. M. Williams and Her Friends,* Paris, 1930.

On Mary Wollstonecraft: William Godwin, *Vie et Mémoires de Mary Wollstonecraft-Godwin,* Paris, 1927; Mary Wollstonecraft, *Love Letters of Mary Wollstonecraft to Gilbert Imlay,* Philadelphia, 1908.

Alicia Church's marriage contract is in the National Archives of France.

On Thomas Paine's retreat to the suburbs of Saint-Denis: Thomas Clio Rickman, *Emigration to America,* London, 1798.

On Genêt in the United States: *American State Papers;* Aulard, *Recueil des actes du Comité de Salut Public;* also, the Annual Report of the American Historical Association, 1897.

## CHAPTER 9

On George Grieve: Maurice Tourneaux, *Bibliographie de l'histoire de Paris,* 1913; Jean Bouchary, *Les Manieurs d'argent à Paris, à la fin du XVIII$^e$ siècle,*

Paris, 1939–1945; the *Mémoire pour George Grieve* and other documents concerning his activities are in the National Archives.

Information on the lives of Mlles. de La Rochefoucauld in the Convent of the British Sisters is taken from William Short's papers. George Sand has described the place in her *History of My Life*.

## CHAPTER 10

On the arrest of American citizens: Alexander Tuetey, *Répertoire général des sources manuscrits de l'histoire de Paris pendant la Révolution française*. The facts concerning Thomas Paine's arrest are contained in the Police Records in the National Archives.

Information on the English spy Monro is in the Public Record Office in London.

## EPILOGUE

On the Wheatcrofts, and Gilbert Imlay's stay in Le Havre: the Municipal Archives in Le Havre.

On Major Jackson: Mathiez, *La Révolution et les étrangers* (cited above, for Chapter 3, on Thomas Paine).

On Gouverneur Morris in Seine-Port: the deed to the property is retained in the National Archives. For an account of the jewelry theft, see the dossier in the Archives of the Police Headquarters.

On William Vans: his autobiography, *Life of William Vans*, in the British Museum; also, *Codman Papers*, Avery Architectural Library of Columbia University, and the Paris Municipal Archives.

# Name Index

Adams, Abigail, 69
Albany, Countess of, 9–10, 181
Alfieri, Vittorio, 10
d'Anville, Duchesse, 10, 50, 63, 122, 197, 202, 203–204
Appleton, Thomas, 31
Armand, Colonel. *See* La Roüerie, Marquis de
d'Arnal, Abbé, 7
d'Artois, Comte, 40, 46, 111–112, 113, 212
Audibert, Achille, 138, 139, 208–209, 210, 213
d'Ayen, Duc, 25, 26

Babcock, Elisha, 21
Bailly, Jean Sylvain, 59, 90, 92
Baldwin, Abraham, 21, 22
Bancal des Issarts, 81, 138, 164, 166, 173, 174, 180
Barclay, Thomas, 6
Barère, 167, 168, 186, 206, 221
Barlow, Joel, 20, 21–22, 23, 25, 31, 36, 46–47, 49, 55, 56, 57, 61, 68–69, 70–71, 79, 91, 135, 140–

141, 143, 144, 145, 146, 147–149, 168, 169, 178, 183, 210–211, 212, 213, 220, 249–250
Barlow, Ruth, 21, 22, 47, 49, 68–70, 79, 91–92, 145, 147–149, 168, 178, 183, 250
Barras, 244, 246
Beaupoil, Jean-Benoît, Comte de Saint-Aulaire, 123, 158, 160, 162
Benoît, 212, 216–217
Beurnonville, Pierre de, 180
Bingham, William, 207, 231
Blackden, Mrs., 32, 68, 129
Blackden, Colonel Samuel, 14, 32–33, 44, 61, 123, 125, 213, 219
Blake, William, 54, 139, 174, 182
Bonnay, President de, 62
Bonneville, Mme. de, 247
Bouret, *Fermier-Général*, 37, 129, 236
Brissac, Duc de, 197
Brissot, Jacques Pierre ("de Warville"), 15, 22, 26, 44, 51, 54, 75, 76, 81, 87, 96, 100, 140, 155,